FREE Test Taking Tips DVD Offer

To help us better serve you, we have developed a Test Taking Tips DVD that we would like to give you for FREE. **This DVD covers world-class test taking tips that you can use to be even more successful when you are taking your test.**

All that we ask is that you email us your feedback about your study guide. Please let us know what you thought about it – whether that is good, bad or indifferent.

To get your **FREE Test Taking Tips DVD**, email freedvd@studyguideteam.com with "FREE DVD" in the subject line and the following information in the body of the email:

> a. The title of your study guide.
>
> b. Your product rating on a scale of 1-5, with 5 being the highest rating.
>
> c. Your feedback about the study guide. What did you think of it?
>
> d. Your full name and shipping address to send your free DVD.

If you have any questions or concerns, please don't hesitate to contact us at freedvd@studyguideteam.com.

Thanks again!

AFOQT Study Guide

AFOQT Test Prep Book Team

Table of Contents

Quick Overview

As you draw closer to taking your exam, effective preparation becomes more and more important. Thankfully, you have this study guide to help you get ready. Use this guide to help keep your studying on track and refer to it often.

This study guide contains several key sections that will help you be successful on your exam. The guide contains tips for what you should do the night before and the day of the test. Also included are test-taking tips. Knowing the right information is not always enough. Many well-prepared test takers struggle with exams. These tips will help equip you to accurately read, assess, and answer test questions.

A large part of the guide is devoted to showing you what content to expect on the exam and to helping you better understand that content. Near the end of this guide is a practice test so that you can see how well you have grasped the content. Then, answers explanations are provided so that you can understand why you missed certain questions.

Don't try to cram the night before you take your exam. This is not a wise strategy for a few reasons. First, your retention of the information will be low. Your time would be better used by reviewing information you already know rather than trying to learn a lot of new information. Second, you will likely become stressed as you try to gain large amount of knowledge in a short amount of time. Third, you will be depriving yourself of sleep. So be sure to go to bed at a reasonable time the night before. Being well-rested helps you focus and remain calm.

Be sure to eat a substantial breakfast the morning of the exam. If you are taking the exam in the afternoon, be sure to have a good lunch as well. Being hungry is distracting and can make it difficult to focus. You have hopefully spent lots of time preparing for the exam. Don't let an empty stomach get in the way of success!

When travelling to the testing center, leave earlier than needed. That way, you have a buffer in case you experience any delays. This will help you remain calm and will keep you from missing your appointment time at the testing center.

Be sure to pace yourself during the exam. Don't try to rush through the exam. There is no need to risk performing poorly on the exam just so you can leave the testing center early. Allow yourself to use all of the allotted time if needed.

Remain positive while taking the exam even if you feel like you are performing poorly. Thinking about the content you should have mastered will not help you perform better on the exam.

Once the exam is complete, take some time to relax. Even if you feel that you need to take the exam again, you will be well served by some down time before you begin studying again. It's often easier to convince yourself to study if you know that it will come with a reward!

Test-Taking Strategies

1. Predicting the Answer

When you feel confident in your preparation for a multiple-choice test, try predicting the answer before reading the answer choices. This is especially useful on questions that test objective factual knowledge or that ask you to fill in a blank. By predicting the answer before reading the available choices, you eliminate the possibility that you will be distracted or led astray by an incorrect answer choice. You will feel much more confident in your selection if you read the question, predict the answer, and then find your prediction among the answer choices. After using this strategy, be sure to still read all of the answer choices carefully and completely. If you feel unprepared, you should not attempt to predict the answers. This would be a waste of time and an opportunity for your mind to wander in the wrong direction.

2. Reading the Whole Question

Too often, test takers scan a multiple-choice question, recognize a few familiar words, and immediately jump to the answer choices. Test authors are aware of this common impatience, and they will sometimes prey upon it. For instance, a test author might subtly turn the question into a negative, or he or she might redirect the focus of the question right at the end. The only way to avoid falling into these traps is to read the entirety of the question carefully before reading the answer choices.

3. Looking for Wrong Answers

Long and complicated multiple-choice questions can be intimidating. One way to simplify a difficult multiple-choice question is to eliminate all of the answer choices that are clearly wrong. In most sets of answers, there will be at least one selection that can be dismissed right away. If the test is administered on paper, the test taker could draw a line through it to indicate that it may be ignored; otherwise, the test taker will have to perform this operation mentally or on scratch paper. In either case, once the obviously incorrect answers have been eliminated, the remaining choices may be considered. Sometimes identifying the clearly wrong answers will give the test taker some information about the correct answer. For instance, if one of the remaining answer choices is a direct opposite of one of the eliminated answer choices, it may well be the correct answer. The opposite of obviously wrong is obviously right! Of course, this is not always the case. Some answers are obviously incorrect simply because they are irrelevant to the question being asked. Still, identifying and eliminating some incorrect answer choices is a good way to simplify a multiple-choice question.

4. Don't Overanalyze

Anxious test takers often overanalyze questions. When you are nervous, your brain will often run wild causing you to make associations and discover clues that don't actually exist. If you feel that this may be a problem for you, do whatever you can to slow down during the test. Try taking a deep breath or counting to ten. As you read and consider the question, restrict yourself to the particular words used by the author. Avoid thought tangents about what the author *really* meant, or what he or she was *trying* to say. The only things that matter on a multiple-choice test are the words that are actually in the question. You must avoid reading too much into a multiple-choice question, or supposing that the writer meant something other than what he or she wrote.

5. No Need for Panic

It is wise to learn as many strategies as possible before taking a multiple-choice test, but it is likely that you will come across a few questions for which you simply don't know the answer. In this situation, avoid panicking. Because most multiple-choice tests include dozens of questions, the relative value of a single wrong answer is small. Moreover, your failure on one question has no effect on your success elsewhere on the test. As much as possible, you should compartmentalize each question on a multiple-choice test. In other words, you should not allow your feelings about one question to affect your success on the others. When you find a question that you either don't understand or don't know how to answer, just take a deep breath and do your best. Read the entire question slowly and carefully. Try rephrasing the question a couple of different ways. Then, read all of the answer choices carefully. After eliminating obviously wrong answers, make a selection and move on to the next question.

6. Confusing Answer Choices

When working on a difficult multiple-choice question, there may be a tendency to focus on the answer choices that are the easiest to understand. Many people, whether consciously or not, gravitate to the answer choices that require the least concentration, knowledge, and memory. This is a mistake. When you come across an answer choice that is confusing, you need to give it extra attention. A question might be confusing because you do not know the subject matter to which it refers. If this is the case, don't eliminate the answer before you have affirmatively settled on another. When you come across an answer choice of this type, set it aside as you look at the remaining choices. If you can confidently assert that one of the other choices is correct, you can leave the confusing answer aside. Otherwise, you will need to take a moment to try to better understand the confusing answer choice. Rephrasing is one way to tease out the sense of a confusing answer choice.

7. Your First Instinct

Many people struggle with multiple-choice tests because they overthink the questions. If you have studied sufficiently for the test, you should be prepared to trust your first instinct once you have carefully and completely read the question and all of the answer choices. There is a great deal of research suggesting that the mind can come to the correct conclusion very quickly once it has obtained all of the relevant information. At times, it may seem to you as if your intuition is working faster even than your reasoning mind. This may in fact be true. The knowledge you obtain while studying may be retrieved from your subconscious before you have a chance to work out the associations that support it. Verify your instinct by working out the reasons that it should be trusted.

8. Key Words

Many test takers struggle with multiple-choice questions because they have poor reading comprehension skills. Quickly reading and understanding a multiple-choice question requires a mixture of skill and experience. To help with this, try jotting down a few key words and phrases on a piece of scrap paper. Doing this concentrates the process of reading and forces the mind to weigh the relative importance of the question's parts. In selecting words and phrases to write down, the test taker thinks about the question more deeply and carefully. This is especially true for multiple-choice questions that are preceded by a long prompt.

9. Subtle Negatives

One of the oldest tricks in the multiple-choice test writer's book is to subtly reverse the meaning of a question with a word like *not* or *except*. If you are not paying attention to each word in the question, you can easily be led astray by this trick. For instance, a common question format is, "Which of the following is...?" Obviously, if the question instead is, "Which of the following is not....?," then the answer will be quite different. Even worse, the test makers are aware of the potential for this mistake and will include one answer choice that would be correct if the question were not negated or reversed. A test taker who misses the reversal will find what he or she believes to be a correct answer and will be so confident that he or she will fail to reread the question and discover the original error. The only way to avoid this is to practice a wide variety of multiple-choice questions and to pay close attention to each and every word.

10. Reading Every Answer Choice

It may seem obvious, but you should always read every one of the answer choices! Too many test takers fall into the habit of scanning the question and assuming that they understand the question because they recognize a few key words. From there, they pick the first answer choice that answers the question they believe they have read. Test takers who read all of the answer choices might discover that one of the latter answer choices is actually *more* correct. Moreover, reading all of the answer choices can remind you of facts related to the question that can help you arrive at the correct answer. Sometimes, a misstatement or incorrect detail in one of the latter answer choices will trigger your memory of the subject and will enable you to find the right answer. Failing to read all of the answer choices is like not reading all of the items on a restaurant menu: you might miss out on the perfect choice.

11. Spot the Hedges

One of the keys to success on multiple-choice tests is paying close attention to every word. This is never more true than with words like *almost*, *most*, *some*, and *sometimes*. These words are called "hedges", because they indicate that a statement is not totally true or not true in every place and time. An absolute statement will contain no hedges, but in many subjects, like literature and history, the answers are not always straightforward or absolute. There are always exceptions to the rules in these subjects. For this reason, you should favor those multiple-choice questions that contain hedging language. The presence of qualifying words indicates that the author is taking special care with his or her words, which is certainly important when composing the right answer. After all, there are many ways to be wrong, but there is only one way to be right! For this reason, it is wise to avoid answers that are absolute when taking a multiple-choice test. An absolute answer is one that says things are either all one way or all another. They often include words like *every*, *always*, *best*, and *never*. If you are taking a multiple-choice test in a subject that doesn't lend itself to absolute answers, be on your guard if you see any of these words.

12. Long Answers

In many subject areas, the answers are not simple. As already mentioned, the right answer often requires hedges. Another common feature of the answers to a complex or subjective question are qualifying clauses, which are groups of words that subtly modify the meaning of the sentence. If the question or answer choice describes a rule to which there are exceptions or the subject matter is complicated, ambiguous, or confusing, the correct answer will require many words in order to be expressed clearly and accurately. In essence, you should not be deterred by answer choices that seem excessively long. Oftentimes, the author of the text will not be able to write the correct answer without offering some qualifications and modifications. As a test taker, your job is to read the answer choices thoroughly and completely and to select the one that most accurately and precisely answers the question.

13. Restating to Understand

Sometimes, a question on a multiple-choice test is difficult not because of what it asks but because of how it is written. If this is the case, restate the question or answer choice in different words. This process serves a couple of important purposes. First, it forces you to concentrate on the core of the question. In order to rephrase the question accurately, you have to understand it well. Rephrasing the question will concentrate your mind on the key words and ideas. Second, it will present the information to your mind in a fresh way. This process may trigger your memory and render some useful scrap of information picked up while studying.

14. True Statements

Sometimes an answer choice will be true in itself, but it does not answer the question. This is one of the main reasons why it is essential to read the question carefully and completely before proceeding to the answer choices. Too often, test takers skip ahead to the answer choices and look for true statements. Having found one of these, they are content to select it without reference to the question above. Obviously, this provides an easy way for test makers to play tricks. The savvy test taker will always read the entire question before turning to the answer choices. Then, having settled on a correct answer choice, he or she will refer to the original question and ensure that the selected answer is relevant. The mistake of choosing a correct-but-irrelevant answer choice is especially common on questions related to specific pieces of objective knowledge, like historical or scientific facts. A prepared test taker will have a wealth of factual knowledge at his or her disposal, and should not be careless in its application.

15. No Patterns

One of the more dangerous ideas that circulates about multiple-choice tests is that the correct answers tend to fall into patterns. These erroneous ideas range from a belief that B and C are the most common right answers, to the idea that an unprepared test-taker should answer "A-B-A-C-A-D-A-B-A." It cannot be emphasized enough that pattern-seeking of this type is exactly the WRONG way to approach a multiple-choice test. To begin with, it is highly unlikely that the test maker will plot the correct answers according to some predetermined pattern. The questions are scrambled and delivered in a random order. Furthermore, even if the test maker was following a pattern in the assignation of correct answers, there is no reason why the test taker would know which pattern he or she was using. Any attempt to discern a pattern in the answer choices is a waste of time and a distraction from the real work of taking the test. A test taker would be much better served by extra preparation before the test than by reliance on a pattern in the answers.

FREE DVD OFFER

Don't forget that doing well on your exam includes both understanding the test content and understanding how to use what you know to do well on the test. We offer a completely FREE Test Taking Tips DVD that covers world class test taking tips that you can use to be even more successful when you are taking your test.

All that we ask is that you email us your feedback about your study guide. To get your **FREE Test Taking Tips DVD**, email freedvd@studyguideteam.com with "FREE DVD" in the subject line and the following information in the body of the email:

- The title of your study guide.
- Your product rating on a scale of 1-5, with 5 being the highest rating.
- Your feedback about the study guide. What did you think of it?
- Your full name and shipping address to send your free DVD.

AFOQT Introduction

Function of the Test

The Air Force Officer Qualifying Test (AFOQT) is a standardized test given by the United States Air Force. The exam evaluates a test taker's verbal and mathematical proficiency as well as his or her aptitude in certain areas specific to those necessary for potential Air Force career paths. The test is used as part of the admissions process to officer training programs, such as Officer Training School ROTC. Within the Air Force, it is used to qualify candidates for Pilot, Combat Systems Officer (CSO), and Air Battle Manager (ABM) training and is part of the Pilot Candidate Selection Method (PCSM) score. The AFOQT is required for all students receiving a scholarship as well as those in the Professional Officer Course (POC).

The test is taken nationwide by current and potential members of the United States Air Force. In the Air Force ROTC program, it is taken by sophomores prior to field training in the summer after their sophomore year.

Test Administration

The AFOQT is offered through Air Force ROTC programs on college campuses and through military recruiters at Military Entrance Processing facilities. There is no cost to take the AFOQT; instead, individuals wishing to take the test must make arrangements through their ROTC program, recruiter, or commanding officer, as appropriate. Rules for retesting depend on the purpose or program for which the test taker is seeking to use the results, but some ROTC programs permit one retest, with the most recent score counting.

Test Format

The test lasts almost five hours, including three hours and 36.5 minutes of testing time and a little over an hour in breaks and test administration time. It is taken with pencil and scored by machine. It consists of twelve subtests: verbal analogies, arithmetic reasoning, word knowledge, math knowledge, reading comprehension, situational judgment, self-description inventory, physical science, table reading, instrument comprehension, block counting, and aviation information. All of the subtests have multiple-choice questions with four or five possible answers.

Scoring

Scores are based only on the number of correct answers. There is no penalty for guessing incorrectly, aside from the missed opportunity to achieve points from a greater number of correct answers. Scores from the various subtests are used to calculate composite scores, which are reported to the test taker and the Air Force. For example, the "Pilot" composite score is based on the results from the arithmetic reasoning, math knowledge, instrument comprehension, table reading, and aviation information subtests. Other composite scores include Academic Aptitude, Verbal, Quantitative, Combat Systems Officer, Air Battle Manager, and Situational Judgment. Test takers receive a percentile score from 1 to 99 in each of the five composite categories.

There is no set passing score. Instead, the scores needed vary widely depending on the intended job or program for which a test taker is seeking entry. For instance, a candidate seeking to become an officer may be able to do so with a relatively low percentile score (in other words, by only outperforming a small number of other test takers), while an officer seeking to become a pilot may need much higher scores overall, particularly in the Pilot composite category.

Recent/Future Developments

The AFOQT is revised from time to time, based on feedback from the general needs of the Air Force and its officer training programs. The current subtests and content therein are in AFOQT Form T, which took effect on August 1, 2014.

A summary of the number of items on and the time allowed for each subtest is as follows:

Subtest	Items	Time (min.)
Verbal Analogies	25	8
Arithmetic Reasoning	25	29
Word Knowledge	25	5
Math Knowledge	25	22
Reading Comprehension	25	38
Situational Judgment	50	35
Self-Description Inventory	240	45
Physical Science	20	10
Table Reading	40	7
Instrument Comprehension	25	5
Block Counting	30	4.5
Aviation Information	20	8
TOTAL	**550**	**3 hours, 36.5 min.**

Verbal Analogies

Verbal Analogies

The verbal analogies test portion of the AFOQT tests the candidate's ability to analyze words carefully and find connections in definition and/or context. The test-taker must compare a selected set of words with answer choices and select the ideal word to complete the sequence. While these exercises draw upon knowledge of vocabulary, this is also a test of critical thinking and reasoning abilities. Naturally, such skills are critical for building a career. Mastering verbal analogies will help people think objectively, discern critical details, and communicate more efficiently.

Question Layout

Verbal analogy sections are on other standardized tests such as the SAT. The format on the AFOQT remains basically the same. First, two words are paired together that provide a frame for the analogy, and then there is a third word that must be found as a match in kind. It may help to think of it like this: A is to B as C is to D. Examine the breakdown below:

Apple (A) is to fruit (B) as carrot (C) is to vegetable (D).

As shown above, there are four words: the first three are given and the fourth word is the answer that must be found. The first two words are given to set up the kind of analogy that is to be replicated for the next pair. We see that apple is paired with fruit. In the first pair, a specific food item, apple, is paired to the food group category it corresponds with, which is fruit. When presented with the third word in the verbal analogy, carrot, a word must be found that best matches carrot in the way that fruit matched with apple. Again, carrot is a specific food item, so a match should be found with the appropriate food group: vegetable! Here's a sample prompt:

Morbid is to dead as jovial is to
    a. Hate.
    b. Fear.
    c. Disgust.
    d. Happiness.
    e. Desperation.

As with the apple and carrot example, here is an analogy frame in the first two words: morbid and dead. Again, this will dictate how the next two words will correlate with one another. The definition of morbid is: described as or appealing to an abnormal and unhealthy interest in disturbing and unpleasant subjects, particularly death and disease. In other words, morbid can mean ghastly or death-like, which is why the word dead is paired with it. Dead relates to morbid because it describes morbid. With this in mind, jovial becomes the focus. Jovial means joyful, so out of all the choices given, the closest answer describing jovial is happiness (D).

Prompts on the exam will be structured just like the one above. "A is to B as C is to ?" will be given, where the answer completes the second pair. Or sometimes, "A is to B as ? is to ?" is given, where the second pair of words must be found that replicate the relationship between the first pair. The only things that will change are the words and the relationships between the words provided.

Discerning the Correct Answer

While it wouldn't hurt in test preparation to expand vocabulary, verbal analogies are all about delving into the words themselves and finding the right connection, the right word that will fit an analogy. People preparing for the test shouldn't think of themselves as human dictionaries, but rather as detectives. Remember, how the first two words are connected dictates the second pair. From there, picking the correct answer or simply eliminating the ones that aren't correct is the best strategy.

Just like a detective, a test-taker needs to carefully examine the first two words of the analogy for clues. It's good to get in the habit of asking the questions: What do the two words have in common? What makes them related or unrelated? How can a similar relationship be replicated with the word I'm given and the answer choices? Here's another example:

Pillage is to steal as meander is to
    a. Stroll.
    b. Burgle.
    c. Cascade.
    d. Accelerate.
    e. Pinnacle.

Why is pillage paired with steal? In this example, pillage and steal are synonymous: they both refer to the act of stealing. This means that the answer is a word that means the same as meander, which is stroll. In this case, the defining relationship in the whole analogy was a similar definition.

What if test-takers don't know what stroll or meander mean, though? Using logic helps to eliminate choices and pick the correct answer. Looking closer into the contexts of the words pillage and steal, here are a few facts: these are things that humans do; and while they are actions, these are not necessarily types of movement. Again, pick a word that will not only match the given word, but best completes the relationship. It wouldn't make sense that burgle (B) would be the correct choice because meander doesn't have anything to do with stealing, so that eliminates burgle. Pinnacle (E) also can be eliminated because this is not an action at all but a position or point of reference. Cascade (C) refers to pouring or falling, usually in the context of a waterfall and not in a reference to people, which means we can eliminate cascade as well. While people do accelerate when they move, they usually do so under additional circumstances: they accelerate while running or driving a car. All three of the words we see in the analogy are actions that can be done independently of other factors. Therefore, accelerate (D) can be eliminated, and stroll (A) should be chosen. Stroll and meander both refer to walking or wandering, so this fits perfectly.

The *process of elimination* will help rule out wrong answers. However, the best way to find the correct answer is simply to differentiate the correct answer from the other choices. For this, test-takers should go back to asking questions, starting with the chief question: What's the connection? There are actually many ways that connections can be found between words. The trick is to look for the answer that is consistent with the relationship between the words given. What is the prevailing connection? Here are a few different ways verbal analogies can be formed.

Finding Connections in Word Analogies

<u>Connections in Categories</u>
One of the easiest ways to choose the correct answer in word analogies is simply to group words together. Ask if the words can be compartmentalized into *distinct categories*. Here are some examples:

Terrier is to dog as mystery is to
  a. Thriller.
  b. Murder.
  c. Detective.
  d. Novel.
  e. Investigation.

This one might have been a little confusing, but when looking at the first two words in the analogy, this is clearly one in which a category is the prevailing theme. Think about it: a terrier is a type of dog. While there are several breeds of dogs that can be categorized as a terrier, in the end, all terriers are still dogs. Therefore, mystery needs to be grouped into a category. Murders, detectives, and investigations can all be involved in a mystery plot, but a murder (B), a detective (C), or an investigation (E) is not necessarily a mystery. A thriller (A) is a purely fictional concept, a kind of story or film, just like a mystery. A thriller can describe a mystery, but same issue appears as the other choices. What about novel (D)? For one thing, it's distinct from all the other terms. A novel isn't a component of a mystery, but a mystery can be a type of novel. The relationship fits: a terrier is a type of dog, just like a mystery is a type of novel.

<u>Synonym/Antonym</u>
Some analogies are based on words meaning the same thing or expressing the same idea. Sometimes it's the complete opposite!

Marauder is to brigand as
  a. King is to peasant.
  b. Juice is to orange.
  c. Soldier is to warrior.
  d. Engine is to engineer.
  e. Paper is to photocopier.

Here, soldier is to warrior (C) is the correct answer. Marauders and brigands are both thieves. They are synonyms. The only pair of words that fits this analogy is soldier and warrior because both terms describe combatants who fight.

Cap is to shoe as jacket is to
  a. Ring.
  b. T-shirt.
  c. Vest.
  d. Glasses.
  e. Pants.

Opposites are at play here because a cap is worn on the head/top of the person, while a shoe is worn on the foot/bottom. A jacket is worn on top of the body too, so the opposite of jacket would be pants (E) because these are worn on the bottom of the body. Often the prompts on the test provide a synonym or antonym relationship. Just consider if the sets in the prompt reflect similarity or stark difference.

Parts of a Whole
Another thing to consider when first looking at an analogy prompt is whether the words presented come together in some way. Do they express parts of the same item? Does one word complete the other? Are they connected by process or function?

Tire is to car as
    a. Wing is to bird.
    b. Oar is to boat.
    c. Box is to shelf.
    d. Hat is to head.
    e. Knife is to sheath.

We know that the tire fits onto the car's wheels and this is what enables the car to drive on roads. The tire is part of the car. This is the same relationship as oar is to boat (B). The oars are attached onto a boat and enable a person to move and navigate the boat on water. At first glance, wing is to bird (A) seems to fit too, since a wing is a part of a bird that enables it to move through the air. However, since a tire and car are not alive and transport people, oar and boat fits better because they are also not alive and they transport people. Subtle differences between answer choices should be found.

Other Relationships
There are a number of other relationships to look for when solving verbal analogies. Some relationships focus on one word being a *characteristic/NOT a characteristic* of the other word. Sometimes the first word is *the source/comprised of* the second word. Still, other words are related by their *location*. Some analogies have *sequential* relationships, and some are *cause/effect* relationships. There are analogies that show *creator/provider* relationships with the *creation/provision*. Another relationship might compare an *object* with its *function* or a *user* with his or her *tool*. An analogy may focus on a *change of grammar* or a *translation of language*. Finally, one word of an analogy may have a relationship to the other word in its *intensity*. The type of relationship between the first two words of the analogy should be determined before continuing to analyze the second set of words. One effective method of determining a relationship between two words is to form a comprehensible sentence using both words and then to plug the answer choices into the same sentence. For example, consider the following analogy: *Bicycle is to handlebars as car is to steering wheel*. A sentence could be formed that says: A bicycle navigates using its handlebars; therefore, a car navigates using its steering wheel. If the second sentence makes sense, then the correct relationship has likely been found. A sentence may be more complex depending on the relationship between the first two words in the analogy. An example of this may be: *food is to dishwasher as dirt is to carwash*. The formed sentence may be: A dishwasher cleans food off of dishes in the same way that a carwash cleans dirt off of a car.

Dealing with Multiple Connections
There are many other ways to draw connections between word sets. Several word choices might form an analogy that would fit the word set in your prompt. When this occurs, the analogy must be explored from multiple angles as, on occasion, multiple answer choices may appear to be correct. When this occurs, ask yourself: which one is an even closer match than the others? The framing word pair is another important point to consider. Can one or both words be interpreted as actions or ideas, or are they purely objects? Here's a question where words could have alternate meanings:

Hammer is to nail as saw is to
- a. Electric.
- b. Hack.
- c. Cut.
- d. Machete.
- e. Groove.

Looking at the question above, it becomes clear that the topic of the analogy involves construction tools. Hammers and nails are used in concert, since the hammer is used to pound the nail. The logical first thing to do is to look for an object that a saw would be used on. Seeing that there is no such object among the answer choices, a test-taker might begin to worry. After all, that seems to be the choice that would complete the analogy – but that doesn't mean it's the only choice that may fit. Encountering questions like this tests one's ability to see multiple connections between words - don't get stuck thinking that words can only be connected in a single way. The first two words given can be verbs instead of just objects. To hammer means to hit or beat; oftentimes it refers to beating something into place. This is also what nail means when it is used as a verb. Here are the word choices that reveal the answer.

First, it's known that a saw, well, saws. It uses a steady motion to cut an object, and indeed to saw means to cut! Cut (C) is one of our answer choices, but the other options should be reviewed. While some tools are electric (a), the use of power in the tools listed in the analogy isn't a factor. Again, it's been established that these word choices are not tools in this context. Therefore, machete (D) is also ruled out because machete is also not a verb. Another important thing to consider is that while a machete is a tool that accomplishes a similar purpose as a saw, the machete is used in a slicing motion rather than a sawing/cutting motion. The verb that describes machete is hack (B), another choice that can be ruled out. A machete is used to hack at foliage. However, a saw does not hack. Groove (E) is just a term that has nothing to do with the other words, so this choice can be eliminated easily. This leaves cut (C), which confirms that this is the word needed to complete the analogy.

Practice Questions

1. **Cat** is to **paws** as
   a. Giraffe is to neck.
   b. Elephant is to ears.
   c. Horse is to hooves.
   d. Snake is to skin.
   e. Turtle is to shell.

2. **Dancing** is to **rhythm** as **singing** is to
   a. Pitch.
   b. Mouth.
   c. Sound.
   d. Volume.
   e. Words.

3. **Towel** is to **dry** as **hat** is to
   a. Cold.
   b. Warm.
   c. Expose.
   d. Cover.
   e. Top.

4. **Sand** is to **glass** as
   a. Protons are to atoms.
   b. Ice is to snow.
   c. Seeds are to plants.
   d. Water is to steam.
   e. Air is to wind.

5. **Design** is to **create** as **allocate** is to
   a. Finish.
   b. Manage.
   c. Multiply.
   d. Find.
   e. Distribute.

6. **Books** are to **reading** as
   a. Movies are to making.
   b. Shows are to watching.
   c. Poetry is to writing.
   d. Scenes are to performing.
   e. Concerts are to music.

7. **Cool** is to **frigid** as **warm** is to
    a. Toasty.
    b. Summer.
    c. Sweltering.
    d. Hot.
    e. Mild.

8. **Buses** are to **rectangular prisms** as **globes** are to
    a. Circles.
    b. Maps.
    c. Wheels.
    d. Spheres.
    e. Movement.

9. **Backpacks** are to **textbooks** as
    a. Houses are to people.
    b. Fences are to trees.
    c. Plates are to food.
    d. Chalkboards are to chalk.
    e. Computers are to mice.

10. **Storm** is to **rainbow** as **sunset** is to
    a. Clouds.
    b. Sunrise.
    c. Breakfast.
    d. Bedtime.
    e. Stars.

11. **Falcon** is to **mice** as **giraffe** is to
    a. Leaves.
    b. Rocks.
    c. Antelope.
    d. Grasslands.
    e. Hamsters.

12. **Car** is to **motorcycle** as **speedboat** is to
    a. Raft.
    b. Jet-ski.
    c. Sailboat.
    d. Plane.
    e. Canoe.

13. **Arid** is to **damp** as **anxious** is to
    a. Happy.
    b. Petrified.
    c. Ireful.
    d. Confident.
    e. Sorrowful.

14. **Mechanic** is to **repair** as
    a. Mongoose is to cobra.
    b. Rider is to bicycle.
    c. Tree is to grow.
    d. Food is to eaten.
    e. Doctor is to heal.

15. **Whistle** is to **blow horn** as **painting** is to
    a. View.
    b. Criticize.
    c. Sculpture.
    d. Painter.
    e. Paintbrush.

16. **Paddle** is to **boat** as **keys** are to
    a. Unlock.
    b. Success.
    c. Illuminate.
    d. Piano.
    e. Keychain.

17. **Monotonous** is to **innovative** as
    a. Gorgeous is to beautiful.
    b. Ancient is to archaic.
    c. Loquacious is to silent.
    d. Sturdy is to fortified.
    e. Spectacular is to grandiose.

18. **Mountain** is to **peak** as **wave** is to
    a. Ocean.
    b. Surf.
    c. Fountain.
    d. Wavelength.
    e. Crest.

19. **Ambiguous** is to **indecisive** as **uncertain** is to
    a. Indefinite.
    b. Certain.
    c. Flippant.
    d. Fearful.
    e. Rounded.

20. **Fluent** is to **communication** as
    a. Crater is to catastrophe.
    b. Gourmet is to cooking.
    c. Ink is to pen.
    d. Crow is to raven.
    e. Whistle is to whistler.

21. **Validate** is to **truth** as **conquer** is to
   a. Withdraw.
   b. Subjugate.
   c. Expand.
   d. Surrender.
   e. Expose.

22. **Winter** is to **autumn** as **summer** is to
   a. Vacation.
   b. Fall.
   c. Spring.
   d. March.
   e. Weather.

23. **Penguin** is to **lemur** as **eagle** is to
   a. Howler monkey.
   b. Osprey.
   c. Warthog.
   d. Kestrel.
   e. Moose.

24. **Fiberglass** is to **surfboard** as
   a. Bamboo is to panda.
   b. Capital is to D.C.
   c. Copper is to penny.
   d. Flint is to mapping.
   e. Wind is to windmill.

25. **Myth** is to **explain** as **joke** is to
   a. Enlighten.
   b. Inspire.
   c. Collect.
   d. Laughter.
   e. Amuse.

Answer Explanations

1. C: This is a part/whole analogy. The common thread is what animals walk on. Choices *A*, *B*, and *E* all describe signature parts of animals, but paws are not the defining feature of cats. While snakes travel on their skins, they do not walk.

2. A: This is a characteristic analogy. The connection lies in what observers will judge a performance on. While the other choices are also important, an off-key singer is as unpleasant as a dancer with no rhythm.

3. D: This is a use/tool analogy. The analogy focuses on an item's use. While hats are worn when it's cold with the goal of making the top of your head warm, this is not always guaranteed—their primary use is to provide cover. There is also the fact that not all hats are used to keep warm, but all hats cover the head.

4. D: This is a source/comprised of analogy. The common thread is addition of fire. Protons contribute to atoms and seeds grow into plants, but these are simple matters of building and growing without necessarily involving fire. B and E relate objects that already have similar properties.

5. E: This is a synonym analogy. The determining factor is synonymous definition. Design and create are synonyms, as are allocate and distribute. Typically, items are found and allocated as part of management to finish a project, but these qualities are not innate in the word. Allocation generally refers to the division of commodities instead of multiplication.

6. B: This is a tool/use analogy. The common thread is audience response to an art form. *A*, *C*, and *D* deal with the creation of artwork instead of its consumption. 6-E describes a form of art instead of the audience engagement with such.

7. C: This is an intensity analogy. The common thread is degree of severity. While *A*, *D*, and *E* can all describe warmth, they don't convey the harshness of sweltering. B simply describes a time when people may be more likely to think of warmth.

8. D: This is a characteristic analogy and is based on matching objects to their geometric shapes. Choice *A* is not correct because globes are three-dimensional, whereas circles exist in two dimensions. While wheels are three-dimensional, they are not always solid or perfectly round.

9. A: This is a tool/use analogy. The key detail of this analogy is the idea of enclosing or sealing items/people. When plates are filled with food, there is no way to enclose the item. While trees can be inside a fence, they can also be specifically outside of one.

10. E: This is a sequence of events analogy. The common thread is celestial cause-and-effect. Not everyone has breakfast or goes to bed after sunset. Sunrise is not typically thought of as the next interesting celestial event after sunsets. While clouds can develop after sunsets, they are also present before and during this activity. Stars, however, can be seen after dark.

11. A: This is a provider/provision analogy. The theme of this analogy is pairing a specific animal to their food source. Falcons prey on mice. Giraffes are herbivores and only eat one of the choices: leaves. Grasslands describe a type of landscape, not a food source for animals.

12. B: This is a category analogy. The common thread is motorized vehicles. While Choices *A*, *C*, and *E* also describe vehicles that move on water, they are not motorized. Although relying on engines, planes are not a form of water transportation.

13. D: This is an antonym analogy. The prevailing connection is opposite meanings. While happy can be an opposite of anxious, it's also possible for someone to experience both emotions at once. *B*, *C*, and *E* are also concurrent with anxious, not opposite.

14. E: This is a provider/provision analogy. This analogy looks at professionals and what their job is. Just as a mechanic's job is to repair machinery, a doctor works to heal patients.

15. C: This is a category analogy. Both whistles and blow horns are devices used to project/produce sound. Therefore, the analogy is based on finding something of a categorical nature. While *A*, *B*, *D*, and *E* involve or describe painting, they do not pertain to a distinct discipline alongside painting. Sculpture, however, is another form of art and expression, just like painting.

16. D: This is a part/whole analogy. This analogy examines the relationship between two objects. Specifically, this analogy examines how one object connects to another object, with the first object(s) being the means by which people use the corresponding object to produce a result directly. People use a paddle to steer a boat, just as pressing keys on a piano produces music. *B* and *C* can be metaphorically linked to keys but are unrelated. *A* is related to keys but is a verb, not another object. 16-E is the trickiest alternative, but what's important to remember is that while keys are connected to key chains, there is no result just by having the key on a key chain.

17. C: This is an antonym analogy. The common thread is opposite meanings. Monotonous refers to being dull or being repetitive, while innovative means new and bringing in changes. All of the other choices reflect synonymous word pairs. However, loquacious, which means talkative, is the opposite of silent.

18. E: This is a part/whole analogy. This analogy focuses on natural formations and their highest points. The peak of a mountain is its highest point just as the crest is the highest rise in a wave.

19. A: This is a negative connotations analogy. Essentially all of the given words in the example express the same idea of uncertainty or not taking a definitive stance. Ambiguous means open to possibilities, which parallels to not being able to make a decision, which describes indecisive as well as uncertain. Uncertain also means not definite, which not only relates to the given words but also directly to indefinite.

20. B: This is an intensity analogy. Fluent refers to how well one can communicate, while gourmet describes a standard of cooking. The analogy draws on degrees of a concept.

21. B: This is a synonym analogy, which relies on matching terms that are most closely connected. Validate refers to finding truth. Therefore, finding the term that best fits conquer is a good strategy. While nations have conquered others to expand their territory, they are ultimately subjugating those lands and people to their will. Therefore, subjugate is the best-fitting answer.

22. C: This is a sequence of events analogy. This analogy pairs one season with the season that precedes it. Winter is paired with autumn because autumn actually comes before winter. Out of all the answers, only *B* and *C* are actual seasons. Fall is another name for autumn, which comes after summer, not before. Spring, of course, is the season that comes before summer, making it the right answer.

23. A: This is a pairs analogy. None the given terms are really related. To find the analogy, the way that each term is paired should be analyzed. Penguin, a bird, is paired with lemur, which is a primate. When given eagle, the only logical analogy to be made is to find another primate to pair with a bird, which is howler monkey.

24. C: This is a source/comprised of analogy. This analogy focuses on pairing a raw material with an object that it's used to create. Fiberglass is used to build surfboards just as copper is used in the creation of pennies. While wind powers a windmill, there is no physical object produced, like with the fiberglass/surfboards pair.

25. E: This is an object/function analogy. The common thread between these words is that one word describes a kind of story and it is paired with the purpose of the story. Myth is/was told in order to explain fundamental beliefs and natural phenomena. While laughter can result from a joke, the purpose of telling a joke is to amuse the audience, thus making *E* the right choice.

Arithmetic Reasoning

The Scope of the Arithmetic Reasoning Section

Problems in the Arithmetic Reasoning section of the AFOQT are generally word problems, which will require the use of reasoning and mathematics to find a solution. The problems normally present some everyday situations, along with a list of choices for answers. Some of the things to know include rates, speeds, percentages, averages, fractions, and ratios. The practice problems given later will cover the different types of questions in this section, although every word problem is slightly different.

How to Prepare

These problems involve basic arithmetic skills as well as the ability to break down a word problem to see where to apply these skills in order to get the correct answer. The basics of arithmetic and the approach to solving word problems are discussed here.

Note that math requires practice in order to become proficient. Make sure to not just read through the material here, but also try out the practice questions, as well as check the answers provided. Just reading through examples does not necessarily mean that a student can do the problems themselves. Note that sometimes there can be multiple approaches to get a solution when doing the problems. What matters is getting the correct answer, so it is okay if the approach to a problem is different than the solution method provided.

Basic Operations of Arithmetic

There are four different basic operations used with numbers: addition, subtraction, multiplication, and division.

- Addition takes two numbers and combines them into a total called the sum. The sum is the total when combining two collections into one. If there are 5 things in one collection and 3 in another, then after combining them, there is a total of $5 + 3 = 8$. Note the order does not matter when adding numbers. For example, $3 + 5 = 8$.

- Subtraction is the opposite (or "inverse") operation to addition. Whereas addition combines two quantities together, subtraction takes one quantity away from another. For example, if there are 20 gallons of fuel and 5 are removed, that gives $20 - 5 = 15$ gallons remaining. Note that for subtraction, the order does matter because it makes a difference which quantity is being removed from which.

- Multiplication is repeated addition. 3×4 can be thought of as putting together 3 sets of items, each set containing 4 items. The total is 12 items. Another way to think of this is to think of each number as the length of one side of a rectangle. If a rectangle is covered in tiles with 3 columns of 4 tiles each, then there are 12 tiles in total. From this, one can see that the answer is the same if the rectangle has 4 rows of 3 tiles each: $4 \times 3 = 12$. By expanding this reasoning, the order the numbers are multiplied does not matter.

- Division is the opposite of multiplication. It means taking one quantity and dividing it into sets the size of the second quantity. If there are 16 sandwiches to be distributed to 4 people, then each person gets $16 \div 4 = 4$ sandwiches. As with subtraction, the order in which the numbers appear does matter for division.

Addition

Addition is the combination of two numbers so their quantities are added together cumulatively. The sign for an addition operation is the + symbol. For example, 9 + 6 = 15. The 9 and 6 combine to achieve a cumulative value, called a sum.

Addition holds the commutative property, which means that numbers in an addition equation can be switched without altering the result. The formula for the commutative property is a + b = b + a. Let's look at a few examples to see how the commutative property works:

$$7 = 3 + 4 = 4 + 3 = 7$$

$$20 = 12 + 8 = 8 + 12 = 20$$

Addition also holds the associative property, which means that the grouping of numbers don't matter in an addition problem. In other words, the presence or absence of parentheses is irrelevant. The formula for the associative property is (a + b) + c = a + (b + c). Here are some examples of the associative property at work:

$$30 = (6 + 14) + 10 = 6 + (14 + 10) = 30$$

$$35 = 8 + (2 + 25) = (8 + 2) + 25 = 35$$

Subtraction

Subtraction is taking away one number from another, so their quantities are reduced. The sign designating a subtraction operation is the − symbol, and the result is called the difference. For example, 9 - 6 = 3. The number *6* detracts from the number *9* to reach the difference *3*.

Unlike addition, subtraction follows neither the commutative nor associative properties. The order and grouping in subtraction impact the result.

$$15 = 22 - 7 \neq 7 - 22 = -15$$

$$3 = (10 - 5) - 2 \neq 10 - (5 - 2) =$$

When working through subtraction problems involving larger numbers, it's necessary to regroup the numbers. Let's work through a practice problem using regrouping:

$$
\begin{array}{r}
3\ 2\ 5 \\
-\ 7\ 7 \\
\hline
\end{array}
$$

Here, it is clear that the ones and tens columns for 77 are greater than the ones and tens columns for 325. To subtract this number, borrow from the tens and hundreds columns. When borrowing from a column, subtracting 1 from the lender column will add 10 to the borrower column:

$$
\begin{array}{r}
{}^{3\text{-}1}\ {}^{10+2\text{-}1}\ {}^{10+5} \\
-\qquad 7\qquad 7 \\
\hline
\end{array}
=
\begin{array}{r}
2\quad 11\quad 15 \\
-\qquad 7\quad 7 \\
\hline
2\quad 4\quad 8
\end{array}
$$

After ensuring that each digit in the top row is greater than the digit in the corresponding bottom row, subtraction can proceed as normal, and the answer is found to be 248.

Multiplication

Multiplication involves adding together multiple copies of a number. It is indicated by an $\times$

symbol or a number immediately outside of a parentheses, e.g. 5(8-2). The two numbers being multiplied together are called factors, and their result is called a product. For example, $9 \times 6 = 54$. This can be shown alternatively by expansion of either the 9 or the 6:

$$9 \times 6 = 9 + 9 + 9 + 9 + 9 + 9 = 54$$

$$9 \times 6 = 6 + 6 + 6 + 6 + 6 + 6 + 6 + 6 + 6 = 54$$

Like addition, multiplication holds the commutative and associative properties:

$$115 = 23 \times 5 = 5 \times 23 = 115$$

$$84 = 3 \times (7 \times 4) = (3 \times 7) \times 4 = 84$$

Multiplication also follows the distributive property, which allows the multiplication to be distributed through parentheses. The formula for distribution is $a \times (b + c) = ab + ac$. This is clear after the examples:

$$45 = 5 \times 9 = 5(3 + 6) = (5 \times 3) + (5 \times 6) = 15 + 30 = 45$$

$$20 = 4 \times 5 = 4(10 - 5) = (4 \times 10) - (4 \times 5) = 40 - 20 = 20$$

Multiplication becomes slightly more complicated when multiplying numbers with decimals. The easiest way to answer these problems is to ignore the decimals and multiply as if they were whole numbers. After multiplying the factors, place a decimal in the product. The placement of the decimal is determined by taking the cumulative number of decimal places in the factors.

For example:

$$0.7 \qquad\qquad 2.6 \qquad\qquad 1.5$$
$$\times\, 3 \qquad\qquad \times\ 4.2 \qquad\qquad \times 6.4$$
$$\overline{ 2.1} \qquad\quad \overline{10.92} \qquad\quad \overline{9.60}$$

Let's tackle the first example. First, ignore the decimal and multiply the numbers as though they were whole numbers to arrive at a product: 21. Second, count the number of digits that follow a decimal (one). Finally, move the decimal place that many positions to the left, as the factors have only one decimal place. The second example works the same way, except that there are two total decimal places in the factors, so the product's decimal is moved two places over. In the third example, the decimal should be moved over two digits, but the digit zero is no longer needed, so it is erased and the final answer is 9.6.

Division

Division and multiplication are inverses of each other in the same way that addition and subtraction are opposites. The signs designating a division operation are the ÷ and / symbols. In division, the second number divides into the first.

The number before the division sign is called the dividend or, if expressed as a fraction, the numerator. For example, in $a \div b$, a is the dividend, while in $\frac{a}{b}$, a is the numerator.

The number after the division sign is called the divisor or, if expressed as a fraction, the denominator. For example, in $a \div b$, b is the divisor, while in $\frac{a}{b}$, b is the denominator.

Like subtraction, division doesn't follow the commutative property, as it matters which number comes before the division sign, and division doesn't follow the associative or distributive properties for the same reason. For example:

$$\frac{3}{2} = 9 \div 6 \neq 6 \div 9 = \frac{2}{3}$$

$$2 = 10 \div 5 = (30 \div 3) \div 5 \neq 30 \div (3 \div 5) = 30 \div \frac{3}{5} = 50$$

$$25 = 20 + 5 = (40 \div 2) + (40 \div 8) \neq 40 \div (2 + 8) = 40 \div 10 = 4$$

If a divisor doesn't divide into a dividend an integer number of times, whatever is left over is termed the remainder. The remainder can be further divided out into decimal form by using long division; however, this doesn't always give a quotient with a finite amount of decimal places, so the remainder can also be expressed as a fraction over the original divisor.

Division with decimals is similar to multiplication with decimals in that when dividing a decimal by a whole number, ignore the decimal and divide as if it were a whole number.

Upon finding the answer, or quotient, place the decimal at the decimal place equal to that in the dividend.

$$15.75 \div 3 = 5.25$$

When the divisor is a decimal number, multiply both the divisor and dividend by 10. Repeat this until the divisor is a whole number, then complete the division operation as described above.

$$17.5 \div 2.5 = 175 \div 25 = 7$$

A *fraction* is a number used to express a ratio. It is written as a number x over a line with another number y underneath: $\frac{x}{y}$, and can be thought of as x out of y equal parts. The number on top (x) is called the *numerator*, and the number on the bottom is called the *denominator* (y). It is important to remember the only restriction is that the denominator is not allowed to be 0.

Another way of thinking about fractions is like this: $\frac{x}{y} = x \div y$.

Two fractions can sometimes equal the same number even when they look different. The value of a fraction will remain equal when multiplying both the numerator and the denominator by the same number. The value of the fraction does not change when dividing both the numerator and the denominator by the same number. For example, $\frac{4}{8} = \frac{2}{4} = \frac{1}{2}$. If two fractions look different, but are actually the same number, these are *equivalent fractions*.

A number that can divide evenly into a second number is called a *divisor* or *factor* of that second number; 3 is a divisor of 6, for example. If the numerator and denominator in a fraction have no common factors other than 1, the fraction is said to be *simplified*. $\frac{2}{4}$ is not simplified (since the numerator and denominator have a factor of 2 in common), but $\frac{1}{2}$ is simplified. Often, when solving a problem, the final answer generally requires us to simplify the fraction.

It is often useful when working with fractions to rewrite them so they have the same denominator. This process is called finding a *common denominator*. The common denominator of two fractions needs to be a number that is a multiple of both denominators. For example, given $\frac{1}{6}$ *and* $\frac{5}{8}$, a common denominator is $6 \times 8 = 48$. However, there are often smaller choices for the common denominator. The smallest number that is a multiple of two numbers is called the *least common multiple* of those numbers. For this example, use the numbers 6 and 8. The multiples of 6 are 6, 12, 18, 24… and the multiples of 8 are 8, 16, 24…, so the least common multiple is 24. The two fractions are rewritten as $\frac{4}{24}, \frac{15}{24}$.

If two fractions have a common denominator, then the numerators can be added or subtracted. For example, $\frac{4}{5} - \frac{3}{5} = \frac{4-3}{5} = \frac{1}{5}$. If the fractions are not given with the same denominator, a common denominator needs to be found before adding or subtracting them.

To multiply two fractions, multiply the numerators to get the new numerator as well as multiply the denominators to get the new denominator. For example, $\frac{3}{5} \times \frac{2}{7} = \frac{3 \times 2}{5 \times 7} = \frac{6}{35}$.

Switching the numerator and denominator is called taking the *reciprocal* of a fraction. So the reciprocal of $\frac{4}{5}$ is $\frac{5}{4}$.

To divide one fraction by another, multiply the first fraction by the reciprocal of the second. So $\frac{3}{4} \div \frac{2}{5} = \frac{3}{4} \times \frac{5}{2} = \frac{15}{8}$.

If the numerator is smaller than the denominator, the fraction is a *proper fraction*. Otherwise, the fraction is said to be *improper*.

A *mixed number* is a number that is an integer plus some proper fraction, and is written with the integer first and the proper fraction to the right of it. Any improper fraction can be rewritten as a mixed number. For instance, $\frac{5}{3} = 1\frac{2}{3}$.

Percentages are essentially just fractions out of 100 (the word comes from the Latin meaning "per one hundred"), and are written with the % symbol. So 35% means $\frac{35}{100}$. Converting from a fraction to a percent requires the fraction to change so it has a denominator of 100; the percent is then the numerator. When converting from a percent to a fraction, it's important to remember that the percent is really a fraction with a denominator of 100.

To convert a decimal to a percent, the decimal point is moved two places to the right. For example, 0.89 = 89%. To convert a percent to a decimal, the decimal point is moved two places to the left. For example, 65% = 0.65.

A *ratio* compares two quantities in size and behaves much like a fraction. If a building has 10 offices and 15 employees, then the ratio of offices to employees is 10 to 15, which can also be written as 10:15. Like fractions, both numbers be can be multiplied or divided in a ratio without changing the value of the ratio. The ratio of offices to employees could also be written as 2 to 3. A ratio is usually given in the form that has the smallest possible whole numbers. As with simplifying fractions, this means the ratio is written using two numbers whose only common factors are 1.

Two quantities are in a *proportional relationship* when one quantity increases or decreases by a fixed fraction of some second quantity. Purchasing gas generally involves a proportional relationship: for each gallon of gas purchased, the price goes up by a fixed amount: Cost = Price × Quantity. All proportional relationships will involve a relationship like this, where one quantity is given by multiplying the second quantity by some factor, which is called the *factor of proportionality*.

Two quantities are in an *inversely proportional* relationship when one quantity decreases as the other increases, in a relationship where the first quantity is given by the second quantity *divided* by some factor. An example of this is the time that a trip takes versus the speed travelled. This is because Time = Distance ÷ Speed. All inversely proportional problems will involve a relationship of this form.

Fractions

A fraction is an equation that represents a part of a whole, but can also be used to present ratios or division problems. An example of a fraction is $\frac{x}{y}$. In this example, x is called the numerator, while y is the denominator. The numerator represents the number of parts, and the denominator is the total number of parts. They are separated by a line or slash. In simple fractions, the numerator and denominator can be nearly any integer. However, the denominator of a fraction can never be zero, because dividing by zero is a function which is undefined.

Imagine that an apple pie has been baked for a holiday party, and the full pie has eight slices. After the party, there are five slices left. How could the amount of the pie that remains be expressed as a fraction? The numerator is 5 since there are two parts left, and the denominator is 8 since there were eight total slices in the whole pie. Thus, expressed as a fraction, the leftover pie totals $\frac{5}{8}$ of the original amount.

Fractions come in three different varieties: proper fractions, improper fractions, and mixed numbers. Proper fractions have a numerator less than the denominator, such as $\frac{3}{8}$, but improper fractions have a numerator greater than the denominator, such as $\frac{15}{8}$. Mixed numbers combine a whole number with a proper fraction, such as $3\frac{1}{2}$. Any mixed number can be written as an improper fraction by multiplying the integer by the denominator, adding the product to the value of the numerator, and dividing the sum by the original denominator. For example, $3\frac{1}{2} = \frac{3\times2+1}{2} = \frac{7}{2}$. Whole numbers can also be converted into fractions by placing the whole number as the numerator and making the denominator 1. For example, $3 = \frac{3}{1}$.

One of the most fundamental concepts of fractions is their ability to be manipulated by multiplication or division. This is possible since $\frac{n}{n} = 1$ for any non-zero integer. As a result, multiplying or dividing by $\frac{n}{n}$ will not alter the original fraction since any number multiplied or divided by 1 doesn't change the value of that number. Fractions of the same value are known as equivalent fractions. For example, $\frac{2}{4}, \frac{4}{8}, \frac{50}{100}$, and $\frac{75}{150}$ are equivalent, as they all equal $\frac{1}{2}$.

Although many equivalent fractions exist, they are easier to compare and interpret when reduced or simplified. The numerator and denominator of a simple fraction will have no factors in common other than 1. When reducing or simplifying fractions, divide the numerator and denominator by the greatest common factor. A simple strategy is to divide the numerator and denominator by low numbers, like 2, 3, or 5 until arriving at a simple fraction, but the same thing could be achieved by determining the greatest common factor for both the numerator and denominator and dividing each by it. Using the first method is preferable when both the numerator and denominator are even, end in 5, or are obviously a multiple of another number. However, if no numbers seem to work, it will be necessary to factor the numerator and denominator to find the GCF. Let's look at examples:

1) Simplify the fraction $\frac{6}{8}$:

Dividing the numerator and denominator by 2 results in $\frac{3}{4}$, which is a simple fraction.

2) Simplify the fraction $\frac{12}{36}$:

Dividing the numerator and denominator by 2 leaves $\frac{6}{18}$. This isn't a simple fraction, as both the numerator and denominator have factors in common. Diving each by 3 results in $\frac{2}{6}$, but this can be further simplified by dividing by 2 to get $\frac{1}{3}$. This is the simplest fraction, as the numerator is 1. In cases like this, multiple division operations can be avoided by determining the greatest common factor between the numerator and denominator.

3) Simplify the fraction $\frac{18}{54}$ by dividing by the greatest common factor:

First, determine the factors for the numerator and denominator. The factors of 18 are 1, 2, 3, 6, 9, and 18. The factors of 54 are 1, 2, 3, 6, 9, 18, 27, and 54. Thus, the greatest common factor is 18. Dividing $\frac{18}{54}$ by 18 leaves $\frac{1}{3}$, which is the simplest fraction. This method takes slightly more work, but it definitively arrives at the simplest fraction.

A ratio is a comparison between the relative sizes of two parts of a whole, separated by a colon. It's different from a fraction because, in a ratio, the second number represents the number of parts which aren't currently being referenced, while in a fraction, the second or bottom number represents the total number of parts in the whole. For example, if 3 pieces of an 8-piece pie were eaten, the number of uneaten parts expressed as a ratio to the number of eaten parts would be 5:3.

Equivalent ratios work just like equivalent fractions. For example, let's find two ratios equivalent to 1:3. Both 3:9 and 20:60 are equivalent ratios because both can be simplified to 1:3.

Operations with Fractions

Of the four basic operations that can be performed on fractions, the one which involves the least amount of work is multiplication. To multiply two fractions, simply multiply the numerators, multiply the denominators, and place the products as a fraction. Whole numbers and mixed numbers can also be expressed as a fraction, as described above, to multiply with a fraction. Let's work through a couple of examples.

$$1)\ \frac{2}{5} \times \frac{3}{4} = \frac{6}{20} = \frac{3}{10}$$

$$2)\ \frac{4}{9} \times \frac{7}{11} = \frac{28}{99}$$

Dividing fractions is similar to multiplication with one key difference. To divide fractions, flip the numerator and denominator of the second fraction, and then proceed as if it were a multiplication problem:

$$1)\ \frac{7}{8} \div \frac{4}{5} = \frac{7}{8} \times \frac{5}{4} = \frac{35}{32}$$

$$2)\ \frac{5}{9} \div \frac{1}{3} = \frac{5}{9} \times \frac{3}{1} = \frac{15}{9} = \frac{5}{3}$$

Addition and subtraction require more steps than multiplication and division, as these operations require the fractions to have the same denominator, also called a common denominator. It is always possible to find a common denominator by multiplying the denominators. However, when the denominators are large numbers, this method is unwieldy, especially if the answer must be provided in its simplest form. Thus, it's beneficial to find the least common denominator of the fractions—the least common denominator is incidentally also the least common multiple.

Once equivalent fractions have been found with common denominators, simply add or subtract the numerators to arrive at the answer:

$$1)\ \frac{1}{2} + \frac{3}{4} = \frac{2}{4} + \frac{3}{4} = \frac{5}{4}$$

$$2)\ \frac{3}{12} + \frac{11}{20} = \frac{15}{60} + \frac{33}{60} = \frac{48}{60} = \frac{4}{5}$$

$$3)\ \frac{7}{9} - \frac{4}{15} = \frac{35}{45} - \frac{12}{45} = \frac{23}{45}$$

$$4)\ \frac{5}{6} - \frac{7}{18} = \frac{15}{18} - \frac{7}{18} = \frac{8}{18} = \frac{4}{9}$$

Percentages

Think of percentages as fractions with a denominator of 100. In fact, percentage means "per hundred." Problems often require converting numbers from percentages, fractions, and decimals. The following explains how to work through those conversions.

Converting Fractions to Percentages: Convert the fraction by using an equivalent fraction with a denominator of 100. For example, $\frac{3}{4} = \frac{3}{4} \times \frac{25}{25} = \frac{75}{100} = 75\%$

Converting Percentages to Fractions: Percentages can be converted to fractions by turning the percentage into a fraction with a denominator of 100. Be wary of questions asking the converted fraction to be written in the simplest form. For example, $35\% = \frac{35}{100}$ which, although correctly written, has a numerator and denominator with a greatest common factor of 5 and can be simplified to $\frac{7}{20}$.

Converting Percentages to Decimals: As a percentage is based on "per hundred," decimals and percentages can be converted by multiplying or dividing by 100. Practically speaking, this always amounts to moving the decimal point two places to the right or left, depending on the conversion. To convert a percentage to a decimal, move the decimal point two places to the right and remove the % sign. To convert a decimal to a percentage, move the decimal point two places to the left and add a "%" sign. Here are some examples:

> 65% = 0.65
> 0.33 = 33%
> 0.215 = 21.5%
> 99.99% = 0.9999
> 500% = 5.00
> 7.55 = 755%

Percentage Problems

Questions dealing with percentages can be difficult when they are phrased as word problems. These word problems almost always come in three varieties. The first type will ask to find what percentage of some number will equal another number. The second asks to determine what number is some percentage of another given number. The third will ask what number another number is a given percentage of.

One of the most important parts of correctly answering percentage word problems is to identify the numerator and the denominator. This fraction can then be converted into a percentage, as described above.

The following word problem shows how to make this conversion:

A department store carries several different types of footwear. The store is currently selling 8 athletic shoes, 7 dress shoes, and 5 sandals. What percentage of the store's footwear are sandals?

First, calculate what serves as the 'whole', as this will be the denominator. How many total pieces of footwear does the store sell? The store sells 20 different types (8 athletic + 7 dress + 5 sandals).

Second, what footwear type is the question specifically asking about? Sandals. Thus, 5 is the numerator.

Third, the resultant fraction must be expressed as a percentage. The first two steps indicate that $\frac{5}{20}$ of the footwear pieces are sandals. This fraction must now be converted into a percentage:

$$\frac{5}{20} \times \frac{5}{5} = \frac{25}{100} = 25\%$$

Basic Geometry Relationships

- The area of a rectangle is lw, where w is the width and l is the length.

- The area of a square is s^2, where s is the length of one side (this follows from the formula for rectangles).

- For a regular prism whose sides are all rectangles, the volume is lwh, where w is the width, l is the length, and h is the height of the prism.

- For a cube, which is a prism whose faces are all squares of the same size, the volume is s^3.

Word Problems

Word problems can appear daunting, but don't let the verbiage psyche you out. No matter the scenario or specifics, the key to answering them is to translate the words into a math problem. Always keep in mind what the question is asking and what operations could lead to that answer.

Translating Words into Math

When asked rewrite a mathematical expression as a situation or translate a word problem into an expression, look for a series of key words indicating addition, subtraction, multiplication, or division:

Addition: add, altogether, together, plus, increased by, more than, in all, sum, and total

Subtraction: minus, less than, difference, decreased by, fewer than, remain, and take away

Multiplication: *times, twice, of, double,* and *triple*

Division: divided by, cut up, half, quotient of, split, and shared equally

Example 1

Alexandra made $96 during the first 3 hours of her shift as a temporary worker at a law office. She will continue to earn money at this rate until she finishes in 5 more hours. How much does Alexandra make per hour? How much will Alexandra have made at the end of the day?

The hourly rate can be figured by dividing $96 by 3 hours to get $32 per hour. Now her total pay can be figured by multiplying $32 per hour by 8 hours, which comes out to $256.

Example 2

Bernard wishes to paint a wall that measures twenty feet wide by eight feet high. It costs ten cents to paint one square foot. How much money will Bernard need for paint?

The final quantity to compute is the *cost* to paint the wall. This will be ten cents ($0.10) for each square foot of area needed to paint. The area to be painted is unknown, but the dimensions of the wall are given; thus, it can be calculated.

The dimensions of the wall are 20 feet wide and 8 feet high. Since the area of a rectangle is length multiplied by width, the area of the wall is 8 x 20 = 160 square feet. Multiplying 0.1 x 160 yields $16 as the cost of the paint

Practice Questions

1. If a car can go 300 miles in 4 hours, how far can it go in an hour and a half?
    a. 100 miles
    b. 112.5 miles
    c. 135.5 miles
    d. 150 miles
    e. 165.5 miles

2. At the store, Jan buys $90 of apples and oranges. Apples cost $1 each and oranges cost $2 each. If Jan buys the same number of apples as oranges, how many oranges did she buy?
    a. 20
    b. 25
    c. 30
    d. 35
    e. 40

3. What is the volume of a box with rectangular sides 5 feet long, 6 feet wide, and 3 feet high?
    a. 60 cubic feet
    b. 75 cubic feet
    c. 90 cubic feet
    d. 100 cubic feet
    e. 115 cubic feet

4. A train traveling 50 miles per hour takes a trip of 3 hours. If a map has a scale of 1 inch per 10 miles, how many inches apart are the train's starting point and ending point on the map?
    a. 10
    b. 12
    c. 13
    d. 14
    e. 15

5. A traveler takes an hour to drive to a museum, spends 3 hours and 30 minutes there, and takes half an hour to drive home. What percentage of this time was spent driving?
    a. 15%
    b. 30%
    c. 40%
    d. 50%
    e. 60%

6. A truck is carrying three cylindrical barrels. Their bases have a diameter of 2 feet and they have a height of 3 feet. What is the total volume of the three barrels in cubic feet?
    a. 3π
    b. 9π
    c. 12π
    d. 15π
    e. 36π

7. Greg buys a $10 lunch with 5% sales tax. He leaves a $2 tip after his bill. How much money does he spend?
   a. $12
   b. $12.50
   c. $13
   d. $13.25
   e. $16

8. Marty wishes to save $150 over a 4-day period. How much must Marty save each day on average?
   a. $33.50
   b. $35
   c. $37.50
   d. $40
   e. $45.75

9. Bernard can make $80 per day. If he needs to make $300 and only works full days, how many days will this take?
   a. 2
   b. 3
   c. 4
   d. 5
   e. 6

10. A couple buys a house for $150,000. They sell it for $165,000. What percentage did the house's value increase?
   a. 10%
   b. 13%
   c. 15%
   d. 17%
   e. 19%

11. A school has 15 teachers and 20 teaching assistants. They have 200 students. What is the ratio of faculty to students?
   a. 3:20
   b. 4:17
   c. 11:54
   d. 3:2
   e. 7:40

12. A map has a scale of 1 inch per 5 miles. A car can travel 60 miles per hour. If the distance from the start to the destination is 3 inches on the map, how long will it take the car to make the trip?
   a. 12 minutes
   b. 15 minutes
   c. 17 minutes
   d. 20 minutes
   e. 25 minutes

13. Taylor works two jobs. The first pays $20,000 per year. The second pays $10,000 per year. She donates 15% of her income to charity. How much does she donate each year?

    a. $4500

    b. $5000

    c. $5500

    d. $6000

    e. $6500

14. A box with rectangular sides is 24 inches wide, 18 inches deep, and 12 inches high. What is the volume of the box in cubic feet?

    a. 2

    b. 3

    c. 4

    d. 5

    e. 6

15. Kristen purchases $100 worth of CDs and DVDs. The CDs cost $10 each and the DVDs cost $15. If she bought four DVDs, how many CDs did she buy?

    a. One

    b. Two

    c. Three

    d. Four

    e. Five

Answer Explanations

1. B: 300 miles in 4 hours is 300/4 = 75 miles per hour. In 1.5 hours, it will go 1.5×75 miles, or 112.5 miles

2. C: One apple/orange pair costs $3 total. Jan therefore bought 90/3 = 30 total pairs, and hence 30 oranges.

3. C: The volume of a box with rectangular sides is the length times width times height, so $5 \times 6 \times 3 = 90$ cubic feet.

4. E: First, the train's journey in the real word is 3 x 50 = 150 miles. On the map, 1 inch corresponds to 10 miles, so there is 150/10 = 15 inches on the map.

5. B: The total trip time is 1 + 3.5 + 0.5 = 5 hours. The total time driving is 1 + 0.5 = 1.5 hours. So the fraction of time spent driving is 1.5/5 or 3/10. To get the percentage, convert this to a fraction out of 100. The numerator and denominator are multiplied by 10, with a result of 30/100. The percentage is the numerator in a fraction out of 100, so 30%.

6. B: The volume of a cylinder is $\pi r^2 h$, where r is the radius and h is the height. The diameter is twice the radius, so these barrels have a radius of 1 foot. That means each barrel has a volume of $\pi 1^2 3 = 3\pi$ cubic feet. Since there are three of them, the total is $3 \times 3\pi = 9$ cubic feet.

7. B: The tip is not taxed, so he pays 5% tax only on the $10. 5% of $10 is $0.05 \times 10 = \$0.50$. Add up $10 + $2 + $0.50 to get $12.50.

8. C: The first step is to divide up $150 into four equal parts. 150/4 is 37.5, so she needs to save $37.50 per day on average.

9. C: 300/80 =30/8 = 15/4 =3.75. But Bernard is only working full days, so he will need to work 4 days, since 3 days is not sufficient.

10. A: The value went up by $165,000 − $150,000 = $15,000. Out of $150,000, this is $\frac{15,000}{150,000} = \frac{1}{10}$. Convert this to having a denominator of 100, the result is $\frac{10}{100}$ or 10%.

11. E: The total faculty is 15 + 20 = 35. So the ratio is 35:200. Then, divide both of these numbers by 5, since 5 is a common factor to both, with a result of 7:40.

12. B: The journey will be $5 \times 3 = 15$ miles. A car travelling at 60 miles per hour is travelling at 1 mile per minute. So it will take 15/1 = 15 minutes to take the journey.

13. A: Taylor's total income is $20,000 + $10,000 = $30,000. 15% of this is $\frac{15}{100} = \frac{3}{20}$. So $\frac{3}{20} \times \$30,000 = \frac{90,000}{20} = \frac{9000}{2} = \$4500$.

14. B: Since the answer will be in cubic feet rather than inches, start by converting from inches to feet for the dimensions of the box. There are 12 inches per foot, so the box is 24/12 = 2 feet wide, 18/12 = 1.5 feet deep, and 12/12 = 1 foot high. The volume is the product of these three together: $2 \times 1.5 \times 1 = 3$ cubic feet.

15. D: Kristen bought four DVDs, which would total a cost of $4 \times 15 = \$60$. She spent a total of $100, so she spent $100 − $60 = $40 on CDs. Since they cost $10 each, she must have purchased 40/10 = four CDs.

Word Knowledge

Word Knowledge

Word knowledge is exactly what it sounds like: this portion of the exam is specifically constructed to test vocabulary skills and the ability to discern the best answer that matches the provided word. Unlike verbal analogies, which will test communication skills and problem-solving abilities along with vocabulary, word knowledge questions chiefly test vocabulary knowledge. While logic and reasoning come into play in this section, they are not as heavily emphasized as with the analogies. A prior knowledge of what the words mean is helpful in order to answer correctly. If the meaning of the words is unknown, that's fine, too; strategies should be used to rule out false answers and choose the correct ones. Here are some study strategies for an optimum performance.

Question Format

In contrast to the verbal analogies, word knowledge questions are very simple in construction. Instead of a comparison of words with an underlying connection, the prompt is just a single word. There are no special directions, alternate meanings, or analogies to work with. The objective is to analyze the given word and then choose the answer that means the same thing <u>or is closest in meaning</u> to the given word. Note the example below:

Blustery
- a. Hard
- b. Windy
- c. Mythical
- d. Stony
- e. Corresponding

All of the questions on the AFOQT word knowledge portion will appear exactly like the above sample. This is generally the standard layout throughout other exams, so some test-takers may already be familiar with the structure. The principle remains the same: at the top of the section, clear directions will be given to choose the answer that most precisely defines the given word. In this case, the answer is windy (B), since windy and blustery are synonymous.

Preparation

In truth, there is no set way to prepare for this portion of the exam that will guarantee a perfect score. This is simply because the words used on the test are unpredictable. There is no set list provided to study from. The definition of the provided word needs to be determined on the spot. This sounds challenging, but there are still ways to prepare mentally for this portion of the test. It may help to expand your vocabulary a little each day. Several resources are available, in books and online, that collect words and definitions that tend to show up frequently on standardized tests. Knowledge of words can increase the strength of your vocabulary.

Mindset is key. The meanings of challenging words can often be found by relying on the past experiences of the test-taker to help deduce the correct answer. How? Well, test-takers have been talking their entire lives – knowing words and how words work. It helps to have a positive mindset from the start. It's unlikely that all definitions of words will be known immediately, but the answer can still be found. There are aspects of words that are recognizable to help discern the correct answers and eliminate the incorrect ones. Below are some of the factors that contribute to word meanings.

Word Origins and Roots

Studying a foreign language in school, particularly Latin or any of the romance languages (Latin-influenced), is advantageous. English is a language highly influenced by Latin and Greek words. The roots of much of the English vocabulary have Latin origins; these roots can bind many words together and often allude to a shared definition. Here's an example:

Fervent
    a. Lame
    b. Joyful
    c. Thorough
    d. Boiling
    e. Cunning

Fervent descends from the Latin word, *fervere*, which means "to boil or glow" and figuratively means "impassioned." The Latin root present in the word is *ferv*, which is what gives fervent the definition: showing great warmth and spirit or spirited, hot, glowing. This provides a link to boiling (D) just by root word association, but there's more to analyze. Among the other choices, none relate to fervent. The word lame (A) means crippled, disabled, weak, or inadequate. None of these match with fervent. While being fervent can reflect joy, joyful (B) directly describes "a great state of happiness," while fervent is simply expressing the idea of having very strong feelings – not necessarily joy. Thorough (C) means complete, perfect, painstaking, or with mastery; while something can be done thoroughly and fervently, none of these words match fervent as closely as boiling does. Cunning (E) means crafty, deceiving or with ingenuity or dexterity. Doing something fervently does not necessarily mean it is done with dexterity. Not only does boiling connect in a linguistic way, but also in the way it is used in our language. While boiling can express being physically hot and undergoing a change, boiling is also used to reflect emotional states. People say they are "boiling over" when in heighted emotional states; "boiling mad" is another expression. Boiling, like fervent, also embodies a sense of heightened intensity. This makes boiling the best choice!

The Latin root *ferv* is seen in other words such as fervor, fervid, and even ferment. All of them are connected to and can be described by boil or glow, whether it is in a physical sense or in a metaphorical one. Such patterns can be seen in other word sets as well. Here's another example:

Gracious
    a. Fruitful
    b. Angry
    c. Grateful
    d. Understood
    e. Overheard

This one's a little easier; the answer is grateful (C), because both words mean thankful! Even if the meanings of both words are known, there's a connection found by looking at the beginnings of both words: *gra/grat*. Once again, these words are built on a root that stretches back to classical language. Both terms come from the Latin, *gratis*, which literally means "thanks."

Understanding root words can help identify the meaning in a lot of word choices, and help the test-taker grasp the nature of the given word. Many dictionaries, both in book form and online, offer information on the origins of words, which highlight these roots. When studying for the test, it helps to look up an unfamiliar word for its definition and then check to see if it has a root that can be connected to any other terms.

Pay Attention to Prefixes

The prefix of a word can actually reveal a lot about its definition. Many prefixes are actually Greco-Roman roots as well – but these are more familiar and a lot easier to recognize! When encountering any unfamiliar words, try looking at prefixes to discern the definition and then compare that with the choices. The prefix should be determined to help find the word's meaning. Here's an example question:

Premeditate
 a. Sporadic
 b. Calculated
 c. Interfere
 d. Determined
 e. Noble

With premeditate, there's the common prefix *pre*. This helps draw connections to other words like prepare or preassemble. *Pre* refers to "before, already being, or having already." Meditate means to think or plan. Premeditate means to think or plan beforehand with intent. Therefore, a term that deals with thinking or planning should be found, but also something done in preparation. Among the word choices, noble (E) and determined (D) are both adjectives with no hint of being related to something done before or in preparation. These choices are wrong. Sporadic (A) refers to events happening in irregular patterns, so this is quite the opposite of premeditated. Interfere (C) also has nothing to do with premeditate; it goes counter to premeditate in a way similar to sporadic. Calculated (B), however, fits! A route and the cost of starting a plan can be calculated. Calculated refers to acting with a full awareness of consequences, so inherently planning is involved. In fact, calculated is synonymous with premeditated, thus making it the correct choice. Just by paying attention to a prefix, the doors to a meaning can open to help easily figure out which word would be the best choice. Here's another example.

Regain
 a. Erupt
 b. Ponder
 c. Seek
 d. Recoup
 e. Enamor

Recoup (D) is the right answer. The prefix *re* often appears in front of words to give them the meaning of occurring again. Regain means to repossess something that was lost. Recoup, which also has the *re* prefix, literally means to regain. In this example, both the given word and the answer share the *re* prefix, which makes the pair easy to connect. However, don't rely *only* on prefixes to choose an answer. Make sure to analyze all of the options before marking an answer. Going through the other words in this sample, none of them come close to meaning regain except recoup. After checking to make sure that recoup is the best matching word, then mark it!

Positive Versus Negative Sounding Words

Another tool for the mental toolbox is simply distinguishing whether a word has a positive or negative connotation. Like electrical wires, words carry energy; they are crafted to draw certain attention and to have certain strength to them. Words can be described as positive and uplifting (a stronger word) or they can be negative and scathing (a stronger word). Sometimes they are neutral – having no particular connotation. Distinguishing how a word is supposed to be interpreted will not only help learn its definition, but also draw parallels with word choices. While it's true that words must usually be taken in the context of how they are used, word definitions have inherent meanings as well, meaning that they have a distinct vibe to pick up on. Here is an example.

Excellent
    a. Fair
    b. Optimum
    c. Reasonable
    d. Negative
    e. Agitation

As you know, excellent is a very positive word. It refers to something being better than good, or above average. In this sample, negative (D) and agitation (E) can easily be eliminated because these are both words with negative connotations. Reasonable (C) is more or less a neutral word: it's not bad but it doesn't communicate the higher quality that excellent represents. It's just, well, reasonable. This leaves the possible choices of fair (A) and optimum (B). Or does it? Fair *is* a positive word; it's used to describe things that are good, even beautiful. But in the modern context, fair is defined as good, but somewhat average or just decent: "You did a fairly good job." or, "That was fair." On the other hand, optimum is positive and a stronger word. Optimum describes the most favorable outcome. This makes optimum the best word choice that matches excellent in both strength and connotation. Not only are the two words positive, but they also express the same level of positivity! Here's another sample.

Repulse
    a. Draw
    b. Encumber
    c. Force
    d. Disgust
    e. Magnify

Repulse just sounds negative when said aloud. It is commonly used in the context of something being repulsive, disgusting, or that which is distasteful. It's also defined as an attack that drives people away. This tells us that we need a word that also carries a negative meaning. Magnify (E) is positive, while draw (A) and force (C) are both neutral. Encumber (B) and disgust (D) are negative. Disgust is a stronger negative than encumber. Of all the words given, only disgust directly defines a feeling of distaste and aversion that is synonymous with repulse and matches in both negativity and strength.

Parts of Speech

It is often very helpful to determine the part of speech of a word. Is it an adjective, adverb, noun, or verb, etc.? Often the correct answer will also be the same part of speech as the given word. Isolate the part of speech and what it describes and look for an answer choice that also describes the same part of speech. For example: if the given word is an adverb describing an action word, then look for another adverb describing an action word.

Swiftly
    a. Fast
    b. Quietly
    c. Angry
    d. Sudden
    e. Quickly

Swiftly is an adverb that describes the speed of an action. Angry (C), fast (A), and sudden (D) can be eliminated because they are not adverbs, and quietly (B) can be eliminated because it does not describe speed. This leaves quickly (E), which is the correct answer. Fast and sudden may throw off some test-takers because they both describe speed, but quickly matches more closely because it is an adverb, and swiftly is also an adverb.

Placing the Word in a Sentence

Often it is easier to discern the meaning of a word if it is used in a sentence. If the given word can be used in a sentence, then try replacing it with some of the answer choices to see which words seem to make sense in the same sentence. Here's an example.

Remarkable
    a. Often
    b. Capable
    c. Outstanding
    d. Shining
    e. Excluding

A sentence can be formed with the word remarkable. "My grade point average is remarkable." None of the examples make sense when replacing the word remarkable in the sentence other than the word outstanding (C), so outstanding is the obvious answer. Shining (D) is also a word with a positive connotation, but outstanding fits better in the sentence.

Looking for Relationships

Remember that all except one of the answer choices are wrong. If a close relationship between three or four of the answer choices can be found and not the fourth or fifth, then some of the choices can be eliminated. Sometimes all of the words are related except one; the one that is not related will often be the correct answer. Here is an example.

Outraged
    a. Angry
    b. Empty
    c. Forlorn
    d. Vacated
    e. Lonely

Notice that all of the answer choices have a negative connotation, but four of them are related to being alone or in low numbers. While two answer choices involve emotions—angry (A) and lonely (E), lonely is related to the other wrong answers, so angry is the best choice to match outraged.

Picking the Closest Answer

As the answer choices are reviewed, two scenarios might stand out. An exact definition match might not be found for the given word among the choices, or there are several word choices that can be considered synonymous to the given word. This is intentionally done to test the ability to draw parallels between the words in order to produce an answer that best fits the prompt word. Again, the closest fitting word will be the answer. Even when facing these two circumstances, finding the one word that fits best is the proper strategy. Here's an example:

Insubordination
    a. Cooperative
    b. Disciplined
    c. Rebel
    d. Contagious
    e. Wild

Insubordination refers to a defiance or utter refusal of authority. Looking over the choices, none of these terms provide definite matches to insubordination like insolence, mutiny, or misconduct would. This is fine; the answer doesn't have to be a perfect synonym. The choices don't reflect insubordination in any way, except rebel (C). After all, when rebel is used as a verb, it means to act against authority. It's also used as a noun: someone who goes against authority. Therefore, rebel is the best choice.

As with the verbal analogies section, playing the role of "detective" is the way to go as you may encounter two or even three answer choices that could be considered correct. However, the answer that best fits the prompt word's meaning is the best answer. Choices should be narrowed one word at a time. The least-connected word should be eliminated first and then proceed until one word is left that is the closest synonym.

Sequence
    a. List
    b. Range
    c. Series
    d. Replicate
    e. Iconic

A sequence reflects a particular order in which events or objects follow. The two closest options are list (A) and series (C). Both involve grouping things together, but which fits better? Consider each word more carefully. A list is comprised of items that fit in the same category, but that's really it. A list doesn't have to follow any particular order; it's just a list. On the other hand, a series is defined by events happening in a set order. A series relies on sequence, and a sequence can be described as a series. Thus, series is the correct answer!

Practice Questions

1. DEDUCE
   a. Explain
   b. Win
   c. Reason
   d. Gamble
   e. Undo

2. ELUCIDATE
   a. Learn
   b. Enlighten
   c. Plan
   d. Corroborate
   e. Conscious

3. VERIFY
   a. Criticize
   b. Change
   c. Teach
   d. Substantiate
   e. Resolve

4. INSPIRE
   a. Motivate
   b. Impale
   c. Exercise
   d. Patronize
   e. Collaborate

5. PERCEIVE
   a. Sustain
   b. Collect
   c. Prove
   d. Lead
   e. Comprehend

6. NOMAD
   a. Munching
   b. Propose
   c. Wanderer
   d. Conscientious
   e. Blissful

7. MALEVOLENT
   a. Evil
   b. Concerned
   c. Maximum
   d. Cautious
   e. Crazy

8. PERPLEXED
   a. Annoyed
   b. Vengeful
   c. Injured
   d. Confused
   e. Prepared

9. LYRICAL
   a. Whimsical
   b. Vague
   c. Fruitful
   d. Expressive
   e. Playful

10. BREVITY
   a. Dullness
   b. Dangerous
   c. Brief
   d. Ancient
   e. Calamity

11. IRATE
   a. Anger
   b. Knowledge
   c. Tired
   d. Confused
   e. Taciturn

12. LUXURIOUS
   a. Faded
   b. Bright
   c. Lavish
   d. Inconsiderate
   e. Overwhelming

13. IMMOBILE
   a. Fast
   b. Slow
   c. Eloquent
   d. Vivacious
   e. Sedentary

14. MENDACIOUS
    a. Earnest
    b. Bold
    c. Criminal
    d. Liar
    e. Humorous

15. CHIVALROUS
    a. Fierce
    b. Annoying
    c. Rude
    d. Dangerous
    e. Courteous

16. RETORT
    a. Conversation
    b. Jest
    c. Counter
    d. Flexible
    e. Erudite

17. SUBLIMINAL
    a. Subconscious
    b. Transportation
    c. Underground
    d. Substitute
    e. Penumbral

18. INCITE
    a. Understanding
    b. Illumination
    c. Rally
    d. Judgment
    e. Compose

19. MONIKER
    a. Name
    b. Mockery
    c. Umbrella
    d. Insult
    e. Burden

20. SERENDIPITOUS
    a. Creation
    b. Sympathy
    c. Unfortunate
    d. Calm
    e. Coincidental

21. OVERBEARING
   a. Neglect
   b. Overacting
   c. Clandestine
   d. Formidable
   e. Amicable

22. PREVENT
   a. Avert
   b. Rejoice
   c. Endow
   d. Fulfill
   e. Ensure

23. REPLENISH
   a. Falsify
   b. Hindsight
   c. Dwell
   d. Refresh
   e. Nominate

24. REGALE
   a. Remember
   b. Grow
   c. Outnumber
   d. Entertain
   e. Bore

25. ABATE
   a. Anger
   b. Forlorn
   c. Withdraw
   d. Excellent
   e. Crazed

Answer Explanations

1. C: To deduce something is to figure it out using reason. Although this might cause a win and prompt an explanation to further understanding, the art of deduction is logical reasoning.

2. B: To elucidate, a light is figuratively shined on a previously unknown or confusing subject. This Latin root, *lux* meaning *light*, prominently figures into the solution. Enlighten means to educate, or bring into the light.

3. D: Looking at the Latin word *veritas*, meaning *truth*, will yield a clue as to the meaning of verify. To verify is the act of finding or assessing the truthfulness of something. This usually means amassing evidence to substantiate a claim. Substantiate, of course, means to provide evidence to prove a point.

4. A: If someone is inspired, they are motivated to do something. Someone who is an inspiration motivates others to follow his or her example.

5. E: All the connotations of perceive involve the concept of seeing. Whether figuratively or literally, perceiving implies the act of understanding what is presented. Comprehending is synonymous with this understanding.

6. C: Nomadic tribes are those who, throughout history and even today, prefer to wander their lands instead of settling in any specific place. Wanderer best describes these people.

7. A: Malevolent literally means bad or evil-minded. The clue is also in the Latin root *mal-* that translates to bad.

8. D: Perplexed means baffled or puzzled, which are synonymous with confused.

9. D: Lyrical is used to refer to something being poetic or song-like, characterized by showing enormous imagination and description. While the context of lyrical can be playful or even whimsical, the best choice is expressive, since whatever emotion lyrical may be used to convey in context will be expressive in nature.

10. C: Brevity literally means brief or concise. Note the similar beginnings of brevity and brief—from the Latin *brevis*, meaning brief.

11. A: Irate means being in a state of anger. Clearly this is a negative word that can be paired with another word in kind. The closest word to match this is obviously anger. Research would also reveal that irate comes from the Latin *ira*, which means anger.

12. C: Lavish is a synonym for luxurious—both describe elaborate and/or elegant lifestyles and/or settings.

13. E: Immobile obviously means *not able to move*. The two best selections are *B* and *E*—but slow still implies some form of motion, whereas sedentary has the connotation of being seated and/or inactive for a significant portion of time and/or as a natural tendency.

14. D: Mendacious describes dishonesty or lying in several ways. This is another word of classical lineage. Mendacio in Latin means *liar*. While liar lacks the Latin root, the meanings fit.

15. E: Chivalrous reflects showing respect and courtesy toward others, particularly women.

16. C: Retort is a verb that means *to answer back*, usually in a sharp manner. This term embodies the idea of a response, emphasized by the *re-* prefix meaning *back, again*. While a retort is used in conversations and even as a jest, neither term embodies the idea of addressing someone again. Counter, however, means to respond in opposition when used as a verb.

17. A: Subliminal and subconscious share the Latin prefix *sub-*, meaning under or below, or more commonly used when talking about messages the sender doesn't want the receiver to consciously take note of. The word subliminal means beneath the consciousness. Thus, subconscious is the perfect match.

18. C: Although incite usually has negative connotations, leaders can incite their followers to benevolent actions as well. In both cases, people rally to support a cause.

19. A: While a moniker commonly refers to a title, this is technically a designated name. Monikers can be mockeries, insults, and/or burdens, but none of these are direct forms of a title or identification.

20. E: Events that occur through serendipity happen purely by chance. Serendipitous conveys the idea of something unplanned yet potentially desirable. Coincidental is defined as happening by chance.

21. B: Overbearing refers to domineering or being oppressive. This is emphasized in the *over* prefix, which emphasizes an excess in definitions. This prefix is also seen in overacting. Similar to overbearing, overacting reflects an excess of action.

22. A: The *pre* prefix describes something that occurs before an event. Prevent means to stop something before it happens. This leads to a word that relates to something occurring beforehand and, in a way, is preventive—wanting to stop something. Avert literally means to turn away or ward off an impending circumstance, making it the best fit.

23. D: Refresh is synonymous with replenish. Both words mean to restore or refill. Additionally, these terms do share the *re-* prefix as well.

24. D: Regale literally means to amuse someone with a story. This is a very positive word; the best way to eliminate choices is to look for a term that matches regale in both positive context/sound and definition. Entertain is both a positive word and a synonym of regale.

25. C: Abate is defined as something becoming less intense and fading. The only word that matches abate is withdraw, which means to go back or draw away from a particular position.

Math Knowledge

The Scope of the Math Knowledge Section

The Math Knowledge section of the test involves everything included in the Arithmetic Reasoning section, as well as some additional mathematical operations and techniques. It is, however, much less focused on word problems.

How to Prepare

Although this section of the test will be less focused on word problems, it is still very important to practice the types of problems in this section. As mentioned before, to really learn mathematics, it is important to practice and not just read through instructions. Approach this section the same as the Arithmetic Reasoning: first, read through the study guide here, then try the practice problems, and lastly, compare your answers with the solutions given below. You may utilize a slightly different method for solving a problem since there are sometimes multiple approaches that will work.

Exponents

An exponent is an operation used as shorthand for a number multiplied or divided by itself for a defined number of times.

$$3^7 = 3 \times 3 \times 3 \times 3 \times 3 \times 3 \times 3$$

In this example, the 3 is called the base and the 7 is called the exponent. The exponent is typically expressed as a superscript number near the upper right side of the base, but can also be identified as the number following a caret symbol (^). This operation would be verbally expressed as "3 to the 7th power" or "3 raised to the power of 7." Common exponents are 2 and 3. A base raised to the power of 2 is referred to as having been "squared," while a base raised to the power of 3 is referred to as having been "cubed."

Several special rules apply to exponents. First, the Zero Power Rule finds that any number raised to the zero power equals 1. For example, 100^0, 2^0, $(-3)^0$ and 0^0 all equal 1 because the bases are raised to the zero power.

Second, exponents can be negative. With negative exponents, the equation is expressed as a fraction, as in the following example:

$$3^{-7} = \frac{1}{3^7} = \frac{1}{3 \times 3 \times 3 \times 3 \times 3 \times 3 \times 3}$$

Third, the Power Rule concerns exponents being raised by another exponent. When this occurs, the exponents are multiplied by each other:

$$(x^2)^3 = x^6 = (x^3)^2$$

Fourth, when multiplying two exponents with the same base, the Product Rule requires that the base remains the same and the exponents are added. For example, $a^x \times a^y = a^{x+y}$. Since addition and multiplication are commutative, the two terms being multiplied can be in any order.

$$x^3 x^5 = x^{3+5} = x^8 = x^{5+3} = x^5 x^3$$

Fifth, when dividing two exponents with the same base, the Quotient Rule requires that the base remains the same, but the exponents are subtracted. So, $a^x \div a^y = a^{x-y}$. Since subtraction and division are not commutative, the two terms must remain in order.

$$x^5 x^{-3} = x^{5-3} = x^2 = x^5 \div x^3 = \frac{x^5}{x^3}$$

Additionally, 1 raised to any power is still equal to 1, and any number raised to the power of 1 is equal to itself. In other words, $a^1 = a$ and $14^1 = 14$.

Exponents play an important role in scientific notation to present extremely large or small numbers as follows: $a \times 10^b$. To write the number in scientific notation, the decimal is moved until there is only one digit on the left side of the decimal point, indicating that the number a has a value between 1 and 10. The number of times the decimal moves indicates the exponent to which 10 is raised, here represented by b. If the decimal moves to the left, then b is positive, but if the decimal moves to the right, then b is negative. See the following examples:

$$3,050 = 3.05 \times 10^3$$

$$-777 = -7.77 \times 10^2$$

$$0.000123 = 1.23 \times 10^{-4}$$

$$-0.0525 = -5.25 \times 10^{-2}$$

Roots

The **square root symbol** is expressed as $\sqrt{}$ and is commonly known as the radical. Taking the root of a number is the inverse operation of multiplying that number by itself some amount of times. For example, squaring the number 7 is equal to 7×7, or 49. Finding the square root is the opposite of finding an exponent, as the operation seeks a number that when multiplied by itself equals the number in the square root symbol.

For example, $\sqrt{36}$ = 6 because 6 multiplied by 6 equals 36. Note, the square root of 36 is also -6 since -6 x -6 = 36. This can be indicated using a plus/minus symbol like this: ±6. However, square roots are often just expressed as a positive number for simplicity with it being understood that the true value can be either positive or negative.

Perfect squares are numbers with whole number–square roots. The list of perfect squares begins with 0, 1, 4, 9, 16, 25, 36, 49, 64, 81, and 100.

Determining the square root of imperfect squares requires a calculator to reach an exact figure. It's possible, however, to approximate the answer by finding the two perfect squares that the number fits between. For example, the square root of 40 is between 6 and 7 since the squares of those numbers are 36 and 49, respectively.

Square roots are the most common root operation. If the radical doesn't have a number to the upper left of the symbol $\sqrt{}$, then it's a square root. Sometimes a radical includes a number in the upper left, like $\sqrt[3]{27}$, as in the other common root type—the cube root. Complicated roots like the cube root often require a calculator.

Parentheses

Parentheses separate different parts of an equation, and operations within them should be thought of as taking place before the outside operations take place. Practically, this means that the distinction between what is inside and outside of the parentheses decides the order of operations that the equation follows. Failing to solve operations inside the parentheses before addressing the part of the equation outside of the parentheses will lead to incorrect results.

For example, let's analyze $5 - (3 + 25)$. The addition operation within the parentheses must be solved first. So $3 + 25 = 28$, leaving $5 - (28) = -23$. If this was solve in the incorrect order of operations, the solution might be found to be $5 - 3 + 25 = 2 + 25 = 27$, which would be wrong.

Equations often feature multiple layers of parentheses. To differentiate them, square brackets [ ] and braces { } are used in addition to parentheses. The innermost parentheses must be solved before working outward to larger brackets. For example, in $\{2 \div [5 - (3 + 1)]\}$, solving the innermost parentheses $(3 + 1)$ leaves $\{2 \div [5 - (4)]\}$. $[5 - (4)]$ is now the next smallest, which leaves $\{2 \div [1]\}$ in the final step, and 2 as the answer.

Order of Operations

When solving equations with multiple operations, special rules apply. These rules are known as the Order of Operations. The order is as follows: Parentheses, Exponents, Multiplication and Division from left to right, and Addition and Subtraction from left to right. A popular pneumonic device to help remember the order is Please Excuse My Dear Aunt Sally (PEMDAS). Evaluate the following two problems to understand the Order of Operations:

1) $4 + (3 \times 2)^2 \div 4$

> First, solve the operation within the parentheses: $4 + 6^2 \div 4$.
> Second, solve the exponent: $4 + 36 \div 4$.
> Third, solve the division operation: $4 + 9$.
> Fourth, finish the operation with addition for the answer, 13.

2) $2 \times (6 + 3) \div (2 + 1)^2$

> $2 \times 9 \div (3)^2$
> $2 \times 9 \div 9$
> $18 \div 9$
> 2

Positive and Negative Numbers

<u>Signs</u>
Aside from 0, numbers can be either positive or negative. The sign for a positive number is the plus sign or the + symbol, while the sign for a negative number is minus sign or the − symbol. If a number has no designation, then it's assumed to be positive.

<u>Absolute Values</u>

Both positive and negative numbers are valued according to their distance from 0. Look at this number line for +3 and -3:

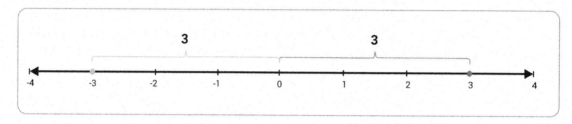

Both 3 and -3 are three spaces from 0. The distance from 0 is called its absolute value. Thus, both -3 and 3 have an absolute value of 3 since they're both three spaces away from 0.

An absolute number is written by placing | | around the number. So, |3| and |−3| both equal 3, as that's their common absolute value.

Implications for Addition and Subtraction

For addition, if all numbers are either positive or negative, simply add them together. For example, 4 + 4 = 8 and -4 + -4 = -8. However, things get tricky when some of the numbers are negative and some are positive.

Take 6 + (-4) as an example. First, take the absolute values of the numbers, which are 6 and 4. Second, subtract the smaller value from the larger. The equation becomes $6 - 4 = 2$. Third, place the sign of the original larger number on the sum. Here, 6 is the larger number, and it's positive, so the sum is 2.

Here's an example where the negative number has a larger absolute value: (-6) + 4. The first two steps are the same as the example above. However, on the third step, the negative sign must be placed on the sum, as the absolute value of (-6) is greater than 4. Thus, -6 + 4 = -2.

The absolute value of numbers implies that subtraction can be thought of as flip the sign of the number following the subtraction sign and simply adding the two numbers. This means that subtracting a negative number will in fact be adding the positive absolute value of the negative number. Here are some examples:

$$-6 - 4 = -6 + -4 = -10$$

$$3 - -6 = 3 + 9 = 12$$

$$-3 - 2 = -3 + -2 = -5$$

Implications for Multiplication and Division

For multiplication and division, if both numbers are positive, then the product or quotient is always positive. If both numbers are negative, then the product or quotient is also positive. However, if the numbers have opposite signs, the product or quotient is always negative.

Simply put, the product in multiplication and quotient in division is always positive, unless the numbers have opposing signs, in which case it's negative.

Here are some examples:

$$(-6) \times (-5) = 30$$

$$(-50) \div 10 = -5$$

$$8 \times |-7| = 56$$

$$(-48) \div (-6) = 8$$

If there are more than two numbers in a multiplication or division problem, then whether the product or quotient is positive or negative depends on the number of negative numbers in the problem. If there is an odd number of negatives, then the product or quotient is negative. If there is an even number of negative numbers, then the result is positive.

Here are some examples:

$$(-6) \times 5 \times (-2) \times (-4) = -240$$

$$(-6) \times 5 \times 2 \times (-4) = 240$$

Polynomials

A *polynomial* is an expression of variables whose exponents are non-negative integers. For example, $6x^5 + 11x^4 + 6x$ is a polynomial, but $\frac{2x}{5x+1}$ is not. As with integers, a polynomial is a *factor* of a second polynomial if the second polynomial can be obtained from the first by multiplication with another polynomial. Finding the factors of a polynomial can be an involved process.

Here are a few rules for factoring polynomials:

1. $x^2 + 2xy + y^2 = (x + y)^2$

2. $x^2 - 2xy + y^2 = (x - y)^2$

3. $x^2 - y^2 = (x + y)(x - y)$

4. $x^3 + y^3 = (x + y)(x^2 - xy + y^2)$

5. $x^3 - y^3 = (x - y)(x^2 + xy + y^2)$

6. $x^3 + 3x^2y + 3xy^2 + y^3 = (x + y)^3$

7. $x^3 - 3x^2y + 3xy^2 - y^3 = (x - y)^3$

Systems of Equations

To start, a review of linear equations is needed. When given a linear equation, the equation will show two expressions containing a variable that must be equal. Thus, one example would be $3x + 1 = 16$. To solve such an equation, remember two things. First, the final solution must equal x. Second, if two quantities are equal, one can add, subtract, multiply, or divide the same thing on both sides and end up with a true equation. In this case, subtract 1 from both sides, which would be a new equation, $3x = 15$. Then, divide both sides by 3 to get $x = 5$.

A system of equations can be solved by the same kinds of considerations, except that in this case, there are multiple equations that all have to be true at the same time. This means there are some new choices for finding solutions. First, if there are two equations, add the left side and the right side to get a new equation (the left side of the new equation is the sum of the left sides, and the right side of the new equation will be the sum of the right sides). Second, if one equation is solved in terms of one of the variables, the expression can be substituted into the other equation. Otherwise, the approach to solving these systems will be similar to solving a single equation.

A system of equations with at least one solution is called a *consistent system*. If a system has no solution, it is called an *inconsistent system*.

A *linear system* of equations with two variables and two equations is a system with variables x and y (or any other pair of variables) and equations that can be simplified to yield $ax + by = c, dx + ey = f$. There are two ways to solve such a system. The first is to solve for one variable in terms of the other and substitute it into the other equation. For example, from the first equation, $by = c - ax$, that means $y = \frac{c-ax}{b}$. $\frac{c-ax}{b}$ can be substituted for y in the second equation. This approach is called solving by *substitution*.

The other possibility is to multiply one of the equations on both sides by some constant, and then add the result to the other equation so that it eliminates one variable. For example, given the pair $ax + by = c, dx + ey = f$, multiply the first equation by $-\frac{d}{a}$. Then the first equation would become $-dx - \frac{db}{a}y = -\frac{cd}{a}$. Adding the equations results in the x terms cancelling, and an equation that only involves the variable y. This approach is called solving by *elimination*.

To illustrate the two approaches, use the system of equations: $2x + 4y = 6, x + y = 2$. This system will be solved using both methods.

By substitution: starting with the second equation, subtract y from both sides. The result of this step is $x = 2 - y$. Substitute $2 - y$ for x in the first equation, with a result of $2(2 - y) + 4y = 6$. This simplifies to $4 - 2y + 4y = 6, 2y = 2, y = 1$. Then, substitute 1 for y into $x = 2 - y$ to find the value for x: $x = 2 - 1 = 1$ or $x = 1$. So $x = 1, y = 1$.

To solve by elimination, starting with $2x + 4y = 6, x + y = 2$: to cancel the $2x$ in the first equation, place a -2x in the second equation on the left. The second equation is then multiplied by -2 on both sides, which gives $-2x - 2y = -4$. The equations are added together: $2x + 4y + (-2x - 2y) = 6 - 4$. The x terms cancel, and the result is $2y = 2$ or $y = 1$. Substituting this back into either of the original equations has a result of $x = 1$. So $x = 1, y = 1$.

Solving for X in Proportions

Proportions are commonly used to solve word problems to find unknown values such as x that are some percent or fraction of a known number. Proportions are solved by cross-multiplying and then dividing to arrive at x. The following examples show how this is done:

1) $\frac{75\%}{90\%} = \frac{25\%}{x}$

To solve for x, the fractions must be cross multiplied: $(75\%x = 90\% \times 25\%)$. To make things easier, let's convert the percentages to decimals: $(0.9 \times 0.25 = 0.225 = 0.75x)$. To get rid of x's co-efficient, each side must be divided by that same coefficient to get the answer $x = 0.3$. The question could ask for the answer as a percentage or fraction in lowest terms, which are 30% and $\frac{3}{10}$, respectively.

2) $\frac{x}{12} = \frac{30}{96}$

Cross-multiply: $96x = 30 \times 12$
Multiply: $96x = 360$
Divide: $x = 360 \div 96$
Answer: $x = 3.75$

3) $\frac{0.5}{3} = \frac{x}{6}$

Cross-multiply: $3x = 0.5 \times 6$
Multiply: $3x = 3$
Divide: $x = 3 \div 3$
Answer: $x = 1$

You may have noticed there's a faster way to arrive at the answer. If there is an obvious operation being performed on the proportion, the same operation can be used on the other side of the proportion to solve for x. For example, in the first practice problem, 75% became 25% when divided by 3, and upon doing the same to 90%, the correct answer of 30% would have been found with much less legwork. However, these questions aren't always so intuitive, so it's a good idea to work through the steps, even if the answer seems apparent from the outset.

FOIL Method

FOIL is a technique for generating polynomials through the multiplication of binomials. A polynomial is an expression of multiple variables (for example, x, y, z) in at least three terms involving only the four basic operations and exponents. FOIL is an acronym for First, Outer, Inner, and Last. *First* represents the multiplication of the terms appearing first in the binomials. *Outer* means multiplying the outermost terms. *Inner* means multiplying the terms inside. *Last* means multiplying the last terms of each binomial.

After completing FOIL and solving the operations, like terms are combined. To identify like terms, look for terms with the same variable and the same exponent. For example, look at $4x^2 - x^2 + 15x + 2x^2 - 8$. The $4x^2, -x^2$, and $2x^2$ are all like terms because they have the variable (x) and exponent (2). Thus, after combining the like terms, the polynomial has been simplified to $5x^2 + 15x - 8$.

The purpose of FOIL is to simplify an equation involving multiple variables and operations. Although it sounds complicated, working through some examples will provide some clarity:

1) Simplify $(x + 10)(x + 4) = (x \times x) + (x \times 4) + (10 \times x) + (10 \times 4)$
$\qquad\qquad\qquad\qquad\qquad\quad$ First $\qquad$ Outer $\qquad$ Inner $\qquad$ Last

After multiplying these binomials, it's time to solve the operations and combine like terms. Thus, the expression becomes: $2x^2 + 4x + 10x + 40 = 2x^2 + 14x + 40$

2) Simplify $2x(4x^3 - 7y^2 + 3x^2 + 4)$

Here, a monomial $(2x)$ is multiplied into a polynomial $(4x^3 - 7y^2 + 3x^2 + 4)$. Using the distributive property, multiply the monomial against each term in the polynomial. This becomes $2x(4x^3) - 2x(7y^2) + 2x(3x^2) + 2x(4)$.

Now, simplify each monomial. Start with the coefficients:

$$(2 \times 4)(x \times x^3) - (2 \times 7)(x \times y^2) + (2 \times 3)(x \times x^2) + (2 \times 4)(x)$$

When multiplying powers with the same base, add their exponents. Remember, a variable with no listed exponent has an exponent of 1, and exponents of distinct variables cannot be combined. This produces the answer:

$$8x^{1+3} - 14xy^2 + 6x^{1+2} + 8x = 8x^4 - 14xy^2 + 6x^3 + 8x$$

3) Simplify $(8x^{10}y^2z^4) \div (4x^2y^4z^7)$

First, divide the coefficients of the first two polynomials: $8 \div 4 = 2$. Second, divide exponents with the same variable, which requires subtracting the exponents. This results in: $2(x^{10-2}y^{2-4}z^{4-7}) = 2x^8y^{-2}z^{-3}$.

However, the most simplified answer should include only positive exponents. Thus, $y^{-2}z^{-3}$ need to be converted into fractions, respectively $\frac{1}{y^2}$ and $\frac{1}{z^3}$. Since the $2x^8$ has a positive exponent, it is placed in the numerator, and $\frac{1}{y^2}$ and $\frac{1}{z^3}$ are combined into the denominator, leaving $\frac{2x^8}{y^2z^3}$ as the final answer.

Geometry and Angles

An *angle* describes the separation or gap between two lines meeting at a single point. It is written with the symbol $\angle$. The point where the lines or line segments meet is called the *vertex* of the angle. If the angle is formed by lines that cross one another, the vertex is the point where they cross.

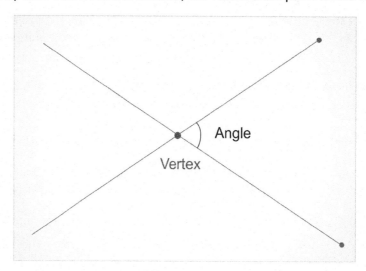

A *right angle* is 90°. An *acute angle* is an angle that is less than 90°. An *obtuse angle* is an angle that is greater than 90° but less than 180°.

An angle of 180° is called a *straight angle*. This is really when two line segments meet at a point, but go in opposite directions, so that they form a single line segment, extending in opposite directions.

A *full angle* is 360°. It means to spin all of the way around from facing one direction back to that same direction. A full circle is considered 360°, or three hundred and sixty *degrees*.

If two angles add together to give 90°, the angles are *complementary*.

If two angles add together to give 180°, the angles are *supplementary*.

When two lines intersect, the pairs of angles they form are always supplementary: the two angles marked here are supplementary:

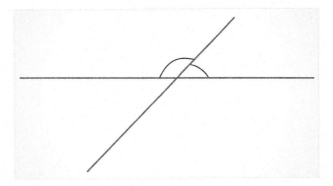

When two supplementary angles are next to one another or "adjacent" in this way, they always give rise to a straight line.

A *triangle* is a geometric shape formed by 3 line segments whose endpoints agree.

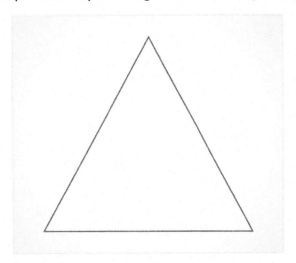

The three angles inside the triangle are called *interior angles* and add up to 180°. Triangles can be classified by the kinds of angles they have and the length of their sides.

An acute triangle is a triangle whose angles are all less than 90°.

If one of the angles in a triangle is 90°, then the triangle is called a *right triangle*.

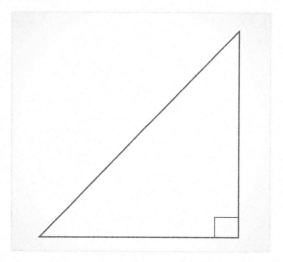

If one of the angles is bigger than 90°, then the triangle is called *obtuse*.

An *isosceles triangle* has two sides of equal length. Equivalently, it has two angles that are the same. It can be acute, right, or obtuse.

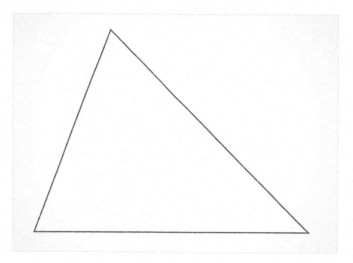

A *scalene triangle* has three sides of different lengths. Equivalently, it has three unequal angles.

An *equilateral triangle* is a triangle whose three sides are the same length. Equivalently, its three angles are equal, and are 60°.

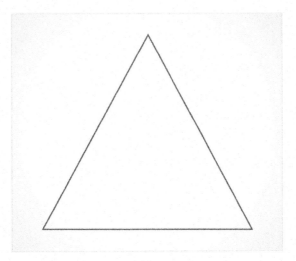

Label the lengths of the sides of a given triangle by A, B, C.

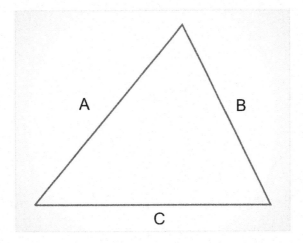

For any triangle, the *Triangle Inequality Theorem* says that the following holds true: $A + B > C, A + C > B, B + C > A$. In addition, the sum of two angles must be less than 180°.

If two triangles have angles that agree with one another, that is, the angles of the first triangle are equal to the angles of the second triangle, then the triangles are called *similar*. Similar triangles look the same, but one can be a "magnification" of the other.

Two triangles with sides that are the same length must also be similar triangles. In this case, such triangles are called *congruent*. Congruent triangles have the same angles and lengths, even if they are rotated from one another.

Practice Questions

1. $\frac{14}{15} + \frac{3}{5} - \frac{1}{30} =$
   a. 19/15
   b. 43/30
   c. 4/3
   d. 3/2
   e. 3

2. Solve for x and y, given $3x + 2y = 8, -x + 3y = 1$.
   a. $x = 2, y = 1$
   b. $x = 1, y = 2$
   c. $x = -1, y = 6$
   d. $x = 3, y = 1$
   e. $x = 4, y = 4$

3. $\frac{1}{2}\sqrt{16} =$
   a. 0
   b. 1
   c. 2
   d. 4
   e. 8

4. The factors of $2x^2 - 8$ are:
   a. $2(4x^2)$
   b. $2(x^2 + 4)$
   c. $2(x + 2)(x + 2)$
   d. $2(x - 2)(x - 2)$
   e. $2(x + 2)(x - 2)$

5. Two of the interior angles of a triangle are 35° and 70°. What is the measure of the last interior angle?
   a. 60°
   b. 75°
   c. 90°
   d. 100°
   e. 105°

6. A square field has an area of 400 square feet. What is its perimeter?
   a. 100 feet
   b. 80 feet
   c. $40\sqrt{2}$ feet
   d. 40 feet
   e. 2 feet

7. $\frac{5}{3} \times \frac{7}{6} =$

    a. $\frac{3}{5}$

    b. $\frac{18}{3}$

    c. $\frac{45}{31}$

    d. $\frac{17}{6}$

    e. $\frac{35}{18}$

8. One apple costs $2. One papaya costs $3. If Samantha spends $35 and gets 15 pieces of fruit, how many papayas did she buy?
    a. Three
    b. Four
    c. Five
    d. Six
    e. Seven

9. If $x^2 - 6 = 30$, then one possible value for x is:
    a. -6
    b. -4
    c. 3
    d. 5
    e. 8

10. A cube has a side length of 6 inches. What is its volume?
    a. 6 cubic inches
    b. 36 cubic inches
    c. 144 cubic inches
    d. 200 cubic inches
    e. 216 cubic inches

11. A square has a side length of 4 inches. A triangle has a base of 2 inches and a height of 8 inches. What is the total area of the square and triangle?
    a. 24 square inches
    b. 28 square inches
    c. 32 square inches
    d. 36 square inches
    e. 40 square inches

12. $-\frac{1}{3}\sqrt{81} =$
    a. -9
    b. -3
    c. 0
    d. 3
    e. 9

13. Simplify $(2x - 3)(4x + 2)$
   a. $8x^2 - 8x - 6$
   b. $6x^2 + 8x - 5$
   c. $-4x^2 - 8x - 1$
   d. $4x^2 - 4x - 6$
   e. $5x^2 + 4x + 3$

14. $\frac{11}{6} - \frac{3}{8} =$
   a. $\frac{5}{4}$

   b. $\frac{51}{36}$

   c. $\frac{35}{24}$

   d. $\frac{3}{2}$

   e. $\frac{39}{16}$

15. A triangle is to have a base 1/3 as long as its height. Its area must be 6 square feet. How long will its base be?
   a. 1 foot
   b. 1.5 feet
   c. 2 feet
   d. 2.5 feet
   e. 3 feet

Answer Explanations

1. D: Start by taking a common denominator of 30. $\frac{14}{15} = \frac{28}{30}, \frac{3}{5} = \frac{18}{30}, \frac{1}{30} = \frac{1}{30}$. Add and subtract the numerators for the next step. $\frac{28}{30} + \frac{18}{30} - \frac{1}{30} = \frac{28+18-1}{30} = \frac{45}{30} = \frac{3}{2}$, where in the last step the 15 is factored out from the numerator and denominator.

2. A: From the second equation, add x to both sides and subtract 1 from both sides: $-x + 3y + x - 1 = 1 + x - 1$, with the result of $3y - 1 = x$. Substitute this into the first equation and get $3(3y - 1) + 2y = 8$, or $9y - 3 + 2y = 8, 11y = 11, y = 1$. Putting this into $3y - 1 = x$ gives $3(1) - 1 = x$ or $x = 2, y = 1$.

3. C: First, the square root of 16 is 4. So this simplifies to $\frac{1}{2}\sqrt{16} = \frac{1}{2}(4) = 2$.

4. E: The easiest way to approach this problem is to factor out a 2 from each term. $2x^2 - 8 = 2(x^2 - 4)$. Use the formula $x^2 - y^2 = (x + y)(x - y)$ to factor $x^2 - 4 = x^2 - 2^2 = (x + 2)(x - 2)$. So $2(x^2 - 4) = 2(x + 2)(x - 2)$.

5. B: The total of the interior angles of a triangle must be 180°. The sum of the first two is 105°, so the remaining is 180° - 105° = 75°.

6. B: The length of the side will be $\sqrt{400}$. The calculation is performed a bit more easily by breaking this into the product of two square roots, $\sqrt{400} = \sqrt{4 \times 100} = \sqrt{4} \times \sqrt{100} = 2 \times 10 = 20$ feet. However, there are 4 sides, so the total is $20 \times 4 = 80$ feet.

7. E: To take the product of two fractions, just multiply the numerators and denominators. $\frac{5}{3} \times \frac{7}{6} = \frac{5 \times 7}{3 \times 6} = \frac{35}{18}$. The numerator and denominator have no common factors, so this is simplified completely.

8. C: Let a be the number of apples purchased, and let p be the number of papayas purchased. There is a total of 15 pieces of fruit, so one equation is $a + p = 15$. The total cost is \$35, and in terms of the total apples and papayas purchased as $2a + 3p = 35$. If we multiply the first equation by 2 on both sides, it becomes $2a + 2p = 30$. We then subtract this equation from the second equation: $2a + 3p - (2a + 2p) = 35 - 30, p = 5$. So five papayas were purchased.

9. A: This equation can be solved as follows: $x^2 = 36$, so $x = \pm\sqrt{36} = \pm 6$. Only -6 shows up in the list.

10. E: The volume of a cube is given by cubing the length of its side. $6^3 = 6 \times 6 \times 6 = 36 \times 6 = 216$.

11. A: The area of the square is the square of its side length, so $4^2 = 16$ square inches. The area of a triangle is half the base times the height, so $\frac{1}{2} \times 2 \times 8 = 8$ square inches. The total is $16 + 8 = 24$ square inches.

12. B: $-\frac{1}{3}\sqrt{81} = -\frac{1}{3}(9) = -3$

13. A: Multiply each of the terms in the first parentheses and then multiply each of the terms in the second parentheses. $(2x - 3)(4x + 2) = 2x(4x) + 2x(2) - 3(4x) - 3(2) = 8x^2 + 4x - 12x - 6 = 8x^2 - 8x - 6$.

14. C: Use a common denominator of 24. $\frac{11}{6} - \frac{3}{8} = \frac{44}{24} - \frac{9}{24} = \frac{44-9}{24} = \frac{35}{24}$.

15. C: The formula for the area of a triangle with base b and height h is $\frac{1}{2}bh$, where the base is one-third the height, or $b = \frac{1}{3}h$ or equivalently $h = 3b$. Using the formula for a triangle, this becomes $\frac{1}{2}b(3b) = \frac{3}{2}b^2$. Now, this has to be equal to 6. So $\frac{3}{2}b^2 = 6, b^2 = 4, b = \pm 2$. However, lengths are positive, so the base must be 2 feet long.

Reading Comprehension

Reading Comprehension

The final English language portion of the AFOQT exam deals with reading comprehension. Like with the previous sections, the Reading Comprehension section will test how well a test-taker grasps words and makes connections, but on a broader scale. A writing sample will be presented to read and analyze, and then questions will need to be answered about the material. The purpose of this is to test how thoroughly and quickly written material can be processed. Unlike the other two sections, though, the answers to the questions are on the pages of the test! It's necessary to read through the selection and find the answers or deduce the proper response from the context. Reading comprehension skills will not only make a better reader but also help to hone analyzing, time management, and critical thinking capabilities.

Question Format

In both the Verbal Analogies and the Word Knowledge sections, prompts were given to make connections between words. Each verbal analogy requires finding a word to complete the sequence, while word knowledge prompts require matching the given word with its definition or closest-fitting synonym. Notice that these are not so much questions as they are prompts. Reading comprehension questions are actually questions that require a complete answer. These questions ask for specific information that must be gleaned from reading a provided text. The task is to read through the provided writing sample and then use that information to answer questions. These questions can either be directly linked to the text itself, such as data, facts, or character information, or the questions can ask for a reflection on the material and then a reasonable response must be chosen. As with other sections of the AFOQT, there's no list of writing materials or set questions that will be presented on the test. While the reading selections are likely to require rigorous reading capabilities and can potentially involve technical or scientific topics, it's not required to have expertise on the subject matter to answer the questions. All of the answers to the questions can be found within the selection, but the answer may not be obvious at first. The questions may involve making judgments about the writing to answer them well. To help with preparation, here are some strategies for sifting through the reading material and the kinds of questions likely to be encountered.

To Read or Not To Read: Strategies for Reading Comprehension

Reading comprehension is comprised of reading a passage but also then going through and carefully choosing answers regarding the content, all within a set time of 39 minutes. The time crunch is a huge part of how this exercise is designed to challenge test-takers. Therefore, using time effectively will definitely influence performance in this section. This, of course, is the first challenge. Clearly, the provided writing sample needs to be addressed, but how much time should actually be spent reading it?

Preparation for this portion of the exam should include an understanding of how quickly and efficiently information can be absorbed and processed. Some people are slow and careful readers, and others are quick and efficient. The ability to swiftly read through a passage entirely and then answer questions accurately is ideal, but this isn't the only way. While the text should definitely be read, poring over it for too long can be troublesome. Not every detail from the writing selection will need to be remembered. A better approach would be to read through the article carefully but swiftly enough to pick out key information and then go to the questions. This is sometimes known as speed-reading. Remember, full access to the article is there to refer back to for answers or for a deeper understanding, when needed. Another approach would be to look over the questions first and then delve into the text. This is a very efficient strategy that will help provide an idea of the information to be looking for. All of the questions in this section are multiple-choice. By reading questions and answer choices first, the correct answer can be located while reading.

Whichever method is chosen, comprehension of the material is vital. A good practice exercise would be to select a passage for reading, whether it is a casual novel or article, and read it carefully but quickly. Then answer the six questions:

- Who is the passage about or who wrote it?
- What is the main point?
- Where does it take place?
- When was the article written or when did the story take place?
- How does the author get his/her point across?
- Why was the passage written?

Learning how to grasp the answers behind these questions, and practicing doing so will provide a firm base from which to address the test questions.

More extensively, distinguishing who the writing sample involves is important, whether it's a first-hand account, a reflective article, or whether the article writer is/was an expert. Is the passage about a specific person or a group of people? It's also important to distinguish who the targeted audience is. While reading through the piece, identify what the focus of the piece is, as most of the comprehension questions will probably ask about this. Identifying where and when the article is set, or if there's a particular location or time period being discussed, is useful for answering specific information questions. The article may be presenting various facts or details about the topic. Pay careful attention to the circumstances of any events being discussed and remember how they happened. Why the selection was written is arguably the most important question to answer and is likely to be among the test questions. While reading, test-takers should question the purpose of the article and consider if the author has a specific goal for his/her writing. Remember that the objective is to identify the most important aspects of the article in order to answer the questions.

Content-Related Questions

Most of the questions encountered will focus directly on the content of the passage. This is where it is important to be able to grasp the essential aspects of the piece. Some of the simpler questions will just ask for facts about the passage. Questions such as these might appear:

- What happened after X occurred?
- Who did X?
- When did the event occur?
- Where did this incident happen?
- In what way did X influence Y?

Questions like these are purely objective; the answers are stated or alluded to in the piece itself. Remember that the content of any article or passage (unless it's fictional) contains evidence and details as well as some writer analysis or speculation. There have to be facts/ideas in the article that cannot be disputed because these are what make up the composition of the article. Read content-related questions carefully and check answers by going over the material again. Unlike the other segments of the AFOQT, the writing passage on this portion of the test will help answer the questions. A good strategy is to pre-read the questions the test asks before reading the selection and then find the information in the selection as you read. Skimming the text might enable the content-related questions to be answered to save time. If the questions focus on recounting specific information from the text, it might be necessary to go back to the writing sample to review. However, carefully reading over the text the first time and noting any answers can save time throughout the process.

Vocabulary-Related Questions

The Reading Comprehension portion of the AFOQT actually combines some aspects of the Verbal Analogies and Word Knowledge sections. All three of the sections build onto each other as they prompt the test-taker to not only identify words but also to draw connections between words. Some questions on the Reading Comprehension section might actually address a word in the text and ask what the word means and how it functions throughout the text. A few questions on the exam might look like these:

- In the first paragraph, *tantalizing* most nearly means what?
- How is *expedite* used to emphasize urgency in the third paragraph?
- In the fifth paragraph, *foreboding* most nearly means what?

These questions not only ask for the identification of word meanings but also how they are used in the context of the whole article. It is asking what the author is trying to communicate through this specific word choice. To answer these questions, look over answer choices and then think about how it was used in the text. If it helps, go to where the word is located in the text and reread the section. Again, this would be a good practice for checking over all of answers, especially if you have time left at the end.

Passage-Reflection Questions

In addition to being able to distinguish important information within the material and answer questions, reading comprehension tests determine how well the passage was interpreted. Many questions will ask for a reflection on the material and choosing the reasonable responses that aren't necessarily found in the article itself. Here are some examples and breakdowns for how to answer them:

<u>What is the purpose of the article?</u>
It needs to be determined if the text is purely informational, if it is an opinion, if it is persuasive, if it illustrates cause and effect, etc. This should be easy to distinguish after reading the passage. What might make answering difficult is the presence of multiple answer choices that seem very close to one another. As with the previous sections of the AFOQT, choosing the best answer that seems most consistent with the writing sample is the proper course of action. It's important to gauge the article's purpose, noting what trends appear more consistently. The author might be trying to educate readers on a new discovery, or persuade them into thinking a particular way. Note if there is an idea constantly focused on or stressed throughout the text. If the writer seems repetitive on something in particular, it could indicate the heart of the author's article, or at least a major focus of the passage. To uncover the purpose of the article, the language and tone of the text should be noted. Look for indicating words or information presented throughout the piece that can help pinpoint the focus of

the article. Examine answer choices and then choose the response that best matches related observations.

What is the tone of the passage?

Tone is usually tied to the purpose of a passage and indicates if the document is serious, educational, persuasive, if it's meant for entertainment, etc. Tone makes readers feel a particular way or indicates what readers should take away from it. The passage might be serious, factual and mostly detail-oriented, or the writing could be somewhat light and casual. Question whether the passage tries to provoke emotion and whether it has a positive or negative connotation. Identifying the tone will help address most, if not all, of the other questions, too. The author's perspective is a key factor in the piece and can lead to another set of possible questions. Here are some examples:

- What is the author's reason for using _____ in the passage?
- Does the author seem to have a distinct view of the events in the text?
- Which of the following statements might the author agree with?

Unless the passage is written in first-person the author's views, motives, tone, or even direct experiences may not be explicitly stated. Unveiling answers to questions like those above require more concentration on the text. These will directly test interpretation and understanding of the writing. In a way, questions like these are asking the readers to go into the mind of the writer and respond from that viewpoint. During an initial reading process, the author's purpose needs to be defined, as this will be the best way to get "in their head." The writing style and evidence presented throughout the text can provide insight into the author's motivations and views. Key details throughout the passage and why the author would include such details in the first place should all be noted.

Examination of the author's word choice and how it reflects emotion and rhetoric is important. It is important to remember, however, that word choice might merely be a way to emphasize facts or points throughout the piece. As the author's motive is revealed while reading, look for indications that could betray a sense of bias in the author's writing. Remember, diction is an important clue in uncovering not only what something means, but also potentially *why* the information in question is described with particular words.

As with all aspects of the AFOQT exam, logic is important. If a question asks for an inference about what would happen after the events of the passage, or if the author would agree with something in particular, the answer that is most consistent with the reading should be chosen. Careful reading of the text helps to gain the necessary insight to answer questions. It's also useful to refer back to the areas of text that emphasized the author's points.

Practice Questions

The next nine questions are based on the following passage.

Sample Passage 1:

Excerpt of *Four Weeks in the Trenches: The War Story of a Violinist*

By Fritz Kreisler

Here we awaited the Russians, and they were not long in coming. First they violently shelled our position and silenced one of our batteries. Finding their artillery fire did not draw any answer from our side, they attempted to storm our position by means of frontal infantry attacks, combined with occasional raids of Cossacks, which were always repulsed. Finally the Russian infantry succeeded in establishing a number of trenches, the one opposite us not more than five hundred yards away. It was the first time we had come in close touch with the Russians, almost within hailing distance, and with the aid of our field glasses we could occasionally even get a glimpse of their faces and recognize their features. We stayed four days opposite each other, neither side gaining a foot of ground.

It was there and then that I made a curious observation. After the second day we had almost grown to know each other. The Russians would laughingly call over to us, and the Austrians would answer. The salient feature of these three days' fighting was the extraordinary lack of hatred. In fact, it is astonishing how little actual hatred exists between fighting men. One fights fiercely and passionately, mass against mass, but as soon as the mass crystallizes itself into human individuals whose features one actually can recognize, hatred almost ceases. Of course, fighting continues, but somehow it loses its fierceness and takes more the form of a sport, each side being eager to get the best of the other. One still shoots at his opponent, but almost regrets when he sees him drop.

By the morning of the third day we knew nearly every member of the opposing trench, the favorite of my men being a giant red-bearded Russian whose constant pastime consisted in jumping like a Jack-in-the-box from the trench, crying over to us as he did so. He was frequently shot at, but never hit. Then he grew bolder, showing himself longer and longer, until finally he jumped out of the trench altogether, shouting to us wildly and waving his cap. His good-humored jollity and bravado appealed to our boys and none of them attempted to shoot at him while he presented such a splendid target. Finally one of our men, who did not want to be second in bravery, jumped out of the trench and presented himself in the full sunlight. Not one attempt was made to shoot at him either, and these two men began to gesticulate at each other, inviting each other to come nearer. All fighting had suddenly ceased, and both opposing parties were looking on, laughing like boys at play. Finally the Russian would draw a step nearer, and our man boldly advanced too. Then the Russians urged on their man with shouts and laughter, and he made a big leap forward, standing still, whereupon the Austrian also jumped forward, and so, step by step, they approached until they nearly touched each other. They had left their rifles behind, and we thought that they were going to indulge in a fist fight, all of us being sorry for our champion, for he was a small and insignificant-looking man who looked as if he could be crushed with one blow by his gigantic opponent. But lo, and behold! The big Russian held out his hand, which held a package of tobacco and our Austrian, seizing the tobacco, grasped the hand of the Russian, and then reaching in his pocket produced a long Austrian cigar, which he ceremoniously presented to the Russian. It was indeed a funny sight to see the small, wiry, lean Austrian talking in exaggerated terms of politeness to the blond Russian giant, who listened gravely and attentively, as if he understood every word.

By this time all precautions and even ideas of fighting had been forgotten, and we were surprised to find ourselves out of the shelter of our trenches and fully exposed to the Russians, who, in turn, leaned out of their own trenches and showed their heads in full. This unofficial truce had lasted about twenty minutes, and succeeded more in restoring good humor and joy of life among our soldiers than a trainload of provisions would have done. It was one of the incidents that helped to relieve the monotony of trench life and was heartily welcomed by all of us. The fighting, however, soon was resumed with all its earnestness and fierceness, but from this moment on, a certain camaraderie was established between the two opposing trenches. Between skirmishes an unofficial truce would frequently be called for the purpose of removing the wounded. During these times when the stretcher-bearers were busy, no shot would be fired on either side.

Nor was this an isolated case, for similar intermittent truces, sometimes accompanied by actual intercourse between the opposing forces, were quite common all along the battle line. That very night I was hurriedly summoned to the trenches of the 13th Company, about half a mile east of us, in order to act as an interpreter between the major commanding that battalion and two singular guests he had just received, a Russian officer and his orderly. The pair, carrying a white flag, had hailed one of the numerous Austrian outposts placed during the night, in front of the trenches, and had been sent blindfolded back to the major. The Russian officer spoke only broken French. He commanded one of the opposing trenches, and from his narrative it appeared that his men had not received any food supplies for some days and were actually on the point of starvation. Not being able to stand their misery any longer, he had taken the bull by the horns and, with the utter confidence and straightforwardness of a fearless nature, had simply come over to us, the enemy, for help, offering a little barrel of water which his companion carried on his head and a little tobacco, in exchange for some provisions. The major seemed at first, perhaps, a little perplexed and undecided about this singular request, but his generous nature and chivalry soon asserted itself. One single look at the emaciated and worn faces of our guests sufficiently substantiated the truth of their story, for both men were utterly exhausted and on the verge of collapse. The next minute messengers were flying to the different trenches of the battalion to solicit and collect contributions, and the officers scrambled over each other in their noble contest to deplete their own last and cherished reserves for the supper of the guests. Soon the latter were seated as comfortably as circumstances permitted before a feast of canned beef, cheese, biscuits, and a slice of salami, my own proud contribution consisting of two tablets of chocolate, part of a precious reserve for extreme cases. It was a strange sight to see these two Russians in an Austrian trench, surrounded by cordiality and tender solicitude. The big brotherhood of humanity had for the time enveloped friend and foe, stamping out all hatred and racial differences. It is wonderful how the most tender flowers of civilization can go hand in hand with the most brutal atrocities of grim modern warfare.

1. What best describes the author of this passage?
    a. A war journalist
    b. An officer recounting his experiences on the front lines
    c. A WWI historian recounting a specific battle
    d. The son of a veteran recounting the stories his father told him
    e. An autobiography of a WWI soldier

2. Which country does the author fight for?
    a. Norway
    b. Italy
    c. Germany
    d. Austria
    e. England

3. What is the distinguishing feature of the enemy soldier whom the author's men come to be friendly with?
    a. One eye is missing.
    b. He has a bald head.
    c. He has a red beard.
    d. He speaks German.
    e. He's very short.

4. What best describes the war in this excerpt?
    a. Pitch battle, very violent
    b. Guerilla warfare from both sides
    c. Heavy casualties are resulting on both sides.
    d. Neither side can even see their opponents.
    e. Both sides are locked in a kind of stalemate; neither side is really gaining an advantage.

5. In the third paragraph, *gesticulate* most nearly means
    a. Offend
    b. Wave
    c. Taunt
    d. Yell
    e. Cower

6. What is the purpose of this passage?
    a. To justify the use of trenches in WWI
    b. To examine the cruelty of the Russian and Austrian troops
    c. To recount war time experience and give perspective on the nature of the warfare
    d. To prove that the Austrian cause was the right one
    e. To persuade the reader to reject war

7. From what the text describes, what can we tell about the Cossacks?
    a. They are allies of the Austrians.
    b. They are working with the Russian forces.
    c. They fight with sabers.
    d. They number only 30 men in order to move quickly and efficiently.
    e. They are mounted warriors.

8. In the fourth paragraph, camaraderie most nearly means:
   a. Trust
   b. Enmity
   c. Uncertainty
   d. Hate
   e. Humor

9. What might the author say about the Russian officer for whom he interpreted?
   a. He was rude and selfish.
   b. The Russian officer was a coward for coming to the Austrians for aid.
   c. He was a brave and honorable officer to come to his enemies for help in order to save his men.
   d. He was treacherous; he betrayed their kindness by stealing all of the Austrian provisions.
   e. He was very warm, telling lots of jokes.

The next nine questions are based on the following passage.

Practice Passage 2:

Includes excerpts from the *Aeneid*

> In the opening lines of the *Aeneid*, we learn that one of the many themes consistent throughout the epic is mercy, or lack thereof. Several of the obstacles Aeneas undergoes are the result of Juno desiring to punish the Trojan people, even after the destruction of their homeland. Aeneas, however, is called to be different, an ideal Roman hero. Thus he is expected not only to lead and judge but to also show mercy, *clementia*. However, throughout the text Aeneas does not always live up to this model, despite the urging of his father, Anchises. There appears to be a reoccurring theme through the text: the idea of failed mercy. We see this both in failing to give reprieve, and also in dire results ensuing from actually showing mercy. It is in the protagonist, Aeneas that we see the most vivid abandonment of *clementia* towards the end of the epic. The prevailing question then becomes whether the instances in which mercy was not shown were actually justified. For Aeneas, there are times when he abandons clemency seemingly out of pure emotional motivations. Yet, it can also be reasoned that past events in the epic and the war Aeneas becomes embroiled in actually influences his decisions to neglect the principle of *clementia* as well. While mercy is an ideal Aeneas is expected to live up to, his lack of mercy reflects necessary action in the war to fulfill his destiny and enact justice after the offences of Turnus.
>
> When Aeneas describes the destruction of Troy, he begins with the deceit of Sinon, the Greek who concealed the true purpose of the Trojan horse to be used as an instrument of Troy's destruction, a device hiding a squad of Greek soldiers that would sack the city. The second factor of Troy's fall came from within the Trojans' own ranks when they were moved to pity for the supplicating Sinon: "Tears won him life, which we granted. We freely gave him our pity." (1. 144-145) In this moment, we see the Trojans acknowledge the supplications of their enemy and spare his life. They do what is expected in their culture and show *clementia* to their defeated prisoner. The diction expresses how they are moved by their pity, which overruled the fact that this man was an enemy. In hindsight this was a major mistake. In giving mercy to Sinon, they ignore the actual deceit that the priest Laocoon warns of. Ironically, the destruction of Troy is the result of mercy, not open warfare. Mercy, in this scenario, was a blinding force that robbed the Trojans of the necessary caution needed towards the enemy:

So spoke Sinon, an artist of perjury, setting his ambush. And we believed him. He fooled us with   well-staged weeping and ruses, conquering men neither Tydeus' son nor Larissa's Achilles, not   even war's ten years and its thousand vessels could vanquish." (2: 195-198)

Showing *clementia* towards the enemy was the catalyst to Troy's final destruction—Aeneas affirms this in the above statement to Dido. Clearly, mercy can prove to have negative outcomes. The betrayal of Sinon is paralleled by some scholars to the historical murderer of Julius Caesar by Brutus, an actual example of how mercy can have ill effect. Julius Caesar himself was famous for his mercy, but like Priam, he was killed for it. Virgil would have been very familiar with this event, as well as the events surrounding Augustus Caesar, Julius' successor, when he learned from his uncle's death (Poulsen 28-38). While Augustus is glorified for ending the civil war of Rome and initiating a lasting peace, it was a feat accomplished with bloodshed. Like Aeneas, Augustus killed those who had killed one he was close with. By defeating Julius Caesar's killers and his personal enemies, Augustus ended the civil war raging in Rome. While vengeance seems to accompany this lack of *clementia* shown on Augustus' enemies, the larger picture cannot be ignored. By vanquishing the opposing forces, Augustus ended the fighting and established a period of peace and growth. If we take this into perspective, then it can also be claimed that Aeneas, likened to Augustus, had to set aside *clementia* for such higher purposes (Poulsen 28-38; Yeomans 30-34).

The noticeable shift in Aeneas' *pietas* (piety) comes in the war with the Latins and the killing of his companion, Pallas. The more the war rages, the more brutal we see Aeneas become, culminating in the final slaying of Turnus. The killing of Pallas by Turnus is clearly a parallel to Achilles in The Iliad after his comrade Partoclus is slain. Aeneas becomes absorbed in grief and violence that overcomes his father's urging to exhibit *clementia*. Book ten displays Aeneas reaping vengeance on everyone aligned with Turnus, even when they supplicate to his humanity. Aeneas' slaying of Magus is the first time we see Aeneas ignoring his father's instruction to show clemency to the defeated: "Spare these multiple masses of silver and gold that you've mentioned, save them for your own sons. This commercial aspect of warfare Turnus was first to suspend just now by his killing of Pallas."(10: 531-533) Despite Magus' offering of goods, Aeneas refuses to be bought by wealth or sympathy, the kind of which spared Sinon. Aeneas does abandon humanity in these moments. He refuses Magus' attempts to seek pity, invoking Aeneas' own sense of fatherhood. Aeneas rejects this and kills him. Now, Aeneas does abandon *clementia*, and he goes on to kill other supplicates before him — but this is not the issue. The issue is *why* and whether the lack of mercy is totally un-warranted. Aeneas' own words give his reasons in the above quote: "This commercial aspect of warfare Turnus was first to suspend just now by his killing of Pallas." Literally, killing Pallas was a last straw. No longer will Aeneas conduct the war in a conventional way or give people the chance to cross him as the Trojans did with Sinon. Now with it being war, Aeneas fully realizes that the men he fights are his true enemies; they just killed his friend and ally. Mercy, sympathy, gold, these all reflect exchange rather than decisive measures in war. A decisive victory is what will ensure his race's survival.

10. What is the best meaning of the Latin word *clementia*?
    a. Peace
    b. Offering
    c. Supplication
    d. Mercy
    e. Rivalry

11. Who was the Greek who the author argues first moved Aeneas to question giving *clementia* to enemies?
    a. Odysseus
    b. Sinon
    c. Magus
    d. Evander
    e. Ulysses

12. What was the purpose of this passage?
    a. To argue that Aeneas' withholding of *clementia* is not a smear on his character, but necessary and   even justified acts within the epic
    b. To prove that Aeneas is not the power hungry conqueror many think of him as
    c. To argue that *clementia* just results in bloodshed
    d. To educate the reader about the Roman virtue of *clementia* and how it can be seen in the *Aeneid*
    e. To prove that Turnus was just a misunderstood character killed wrongly by Aeneas

13. Why does Aeneas kill Magus?
    a. Vengeance for Pallas
    b. He is an enemy soldier and ally of Turnus.
    c. To prove his ferocity
    d. Magus killed his father.
    e. Both A and B are correct.

14. In paragraph 5, *absorbed* means:
    a. Engaged
    b. Interested
    c. Hesitant
    d. Brooding
    e. Meditative

15. What is the connection between Aeneas and Augustus Caesar?
    a. Both were dictators
    b. Both faced similar dilemmas concerning *clementia* and Virgil was likely influenced by Augustus.
    c. Aeneas is, according to legend, a distant ancestor of Julius and Augustus Caesar.
    d. Neither believed in ruling with democracy
    e. Both Aeneas and Augustus inherited Rome.

16. In the quote in paragraph 3, *perjury* most nearly means:
    a. Winning
    b. Crying
    c. Bleeding
    d. Joking
    e. Lying

17. Which statement would the author most agree with?
    a. Aeneas had pure intentions but was corrupted.
    b. Turnus was a threat and needed to die.
    c. Anchises was a sentimental fool.
    d. Aeneas did what was necessary.
    e. Anchises was right about showing *clementia*.

18. In which section of the *Aeneid* does the author first examine Aeneas not giving *clementia* to a fallen foe?
    a. Book 1
    b. Book 10
    c. Book 5
    d. Book 11
    e. Book 3

The next seven questions are based on the following passage.

Practice Passage 3

When researchers and engineers undertake a large-scale scientific project, they may end up making discoveries and developing technologies that have far wider uses than originally intended. This is especially true in NASA, one of the most influential and innovative scientific organizations in America. NASA spinoff technology refers to innovations originally developed for NASA space projects that are now used in a wide range of different commercial fields. Many consumers are unaware that products they are buying are based on NASA research! Spinoff technology proves that it is worthwhile to invest in science research because it could enrich people's lives in unexpected ways.

The first spinoff technology worth mentioning is baby food. In space, where astronauts have limited access to fresh food and fewer options about their daily meals, malnutrition is a serious concern. Consequently, NASA researchers were looking for ways to enhance the nutritional value of astronauts' food. Scientists found that a certain type of algae could be added to food, improving the food's neurological benefits. When experts in the commercial food industry learned of this algae's potential to boost brain health, they were quick to begin their own research. The nutritional substance from algae then developed into a product called Life's DHA, which can be found in over 90% of infant food sold in America.

Another intriguing example of a spinoff technology can be found in fashion. People who are always dropping their sunglasses may have invested in a pair of sunglasses with scratch resistant lenses—that is, it's impossible to scratch the glass, even if the glasses are dropped on an abrasive surface. This innovation is incredibly advantageous for people who are clumsy, but most shoppers don't know that this technology was originally developed by NASA. Scientists first created scratch resistant glass to help protect costly and crucial equipment from getting scratched in space, especially the helmet visors

81

in space suits. However, sunglasses companies later realized that this technology could be profitable for their products, and they licensed the technology from NASA.

19. What is the main purpose of this article?
    a. To advise consumers to do more research before making a purchase
    b. To persuade readers to support NASA research
    c. To tell a narrative about the history of space technology
    d. To define and describe instances of spinoff technology

20. What is the organizational structure of this article?
    a. A general definition followed by more specific examples
    b. A general opinion followed by supporting arguments
    c. An important moment in history followed by chronological details
    d. A popular misconception followed by counterevidence

21. Why did NASA scientists research algae?
    a. They already knew algae was healthy for babies.
    b. They were interested in how to grow food in space.
    c. They were looking for ways to add health benefits to food.
    d. They hoped to use it to protect expensive research equipment.

22. What does the word "neurological" mean in the second paragraph?
    a. Related to the body
    b. Related to the brain
    c. Related to vitamins
    d. Related to technology

23. Why does the author mention space suit helmets?
    a. To give an example of astronaut fashion
    b. To explain where sunglasses got their shape
    c. To explain how astronauts protect their eyes
    d. To give an example of valuable space equipment

24. Which statement would the author probably NOT agree with?
    a. Consumers don't always know the history of the products they are buying.
    b. Sometimes new innovations have unexpected applications.
    c. It is difficult to make money from scientific research.
    d. Space equipment is often very expensive.

25. Which of the following would be the best addition to this passage?
    a. The names of the astronauts involved in the discoveries leading to spinoff technology
    b. A list of some other products that have come about because of NASA spinoff technology
    c. Quotes from consumers who use products that resulted from spinoff technology
    d. A brief history of the funding of NASA

Answer Explanations

1. B: The use of the first person narrative style is a major clue in unveiling who the author is. Clearly this is the story of someone actually experiencing the war firsthand. Specific details also allude that the author is not simply reporting, but actually a fighter in the war and a member of a battalion. In the third paragraph, the author refers to *his men*, an indication that he has some form of command on the field.

2. D: It is very clear that the author is a member of the Austrian army, which is entrenched and fighting the Russian army.

3. C: In the third paragraph, the author describes his men's favorite Russian soldier as being *a giant red-bearded Russian*.

4. E: The author goes on to describe how each side has their own trench line but doesn't talk about how either side is advancing one way or the other: all they can do is fire at one another, but only occasionally. There are also frequent truces and moments of amiable interactions that do not convey a sense of intense violence at that time.

5. B: Looking at the passage, the author recalls how an enemy Russian soldier and Austrian soldier were trying to get one another to approach in a peaceful way and meet; the two soldiers were waving and making motions inviting one another over. Wave is actually a synonym of gesticulate.

6. C: The author is not demeaning the enemy Russians nor is he trying to make the Austrians seem ideal; he's just reporting what he saw on the front. While the author doesn't seem to be overly in favor of the fighting, and indicates that between the individuals there's really nothing to fight over, he doesn't explicitly speak against the war. He merely tells of his experiences and offers reflection. We can infer that he no longer sees the sense in the war, but the text itself doesn't carry an anti-war agenda. This makes C the best choice.

7. B: This particular excerpt does not reveal many details about the Cossacks. The only thing that is clear about them in this section is that they are working with the Russian army to attack the Austrian's position.

8. A: This use of camaraderie reflects the bonds of respect and mutual trust these "enemies" have for each other to the point that both sides allow truces for the wounded on both sides to be treated, trusting one another not to fire while stretcher-bearers go out into the open to tend them.

9. C: In the fifth paragraph, the author makes it clear that he highly respects the Russian officer, describing him as straightforward and fearless: "He had taken the bull by the horns and, with the utter confidence and straightforwardness of a fearless nature, had simply come over to us, the enemy, for help, offering a little barrel of water which his companion carried on his head and a little tobacco, in exchange for some provisions." The author and the other Austrian officers respect the Russian officer so much for caring about his men that they welcome him and exchange supplies as he requested.

10. D: As defined in the first paragraph, *clementia* is the Latin word meaning 'mercy', a concept held in high regard in the *Aeneid*.

11. B: As indicated in the second and third paragraphs, Sinon is the Greek who lied about the Trojan horse, which hid Greek soldiers in it who sacked Troy. After being swayed by pity, the Trojans spared his life, thus showing *clementia* and also sealing their fate. By showing *clementia* to Sinon and believing his story, the Trojans were betrayed and the city fell. Aeneas remembers this throughout his journey and is now more guarded in wartime.

12. A: While the author does explain *clementia* and hints to Aeneas about having inherently good intentions, the primary objective of the piece is to prove that Aeneas had to withhold *clementia* in the *Aeneid*. The author argues that this was not done for purely emotional reasons, but because of human necessity. The author also cites much evidence to support his thesis.

13. E: Magus represents one of the first enemies Aeneas kills without showing *clementia*, even as the enemy begs it of him. While vengeance is a major motivating force for Aeneas, the author elaborates that as a warrior in a war, Aeneas kills Magus to be decisive in battle and to forgo any ceremony to ensure no foul play and a total victory.

14. A: Absorbed is defined as intensely engaged. The term reflects how Aeneas is consumed by grief over the death of Pallas as well as the violence of intense warfare.

15. B: The author mentions Augustus Caesar to provide historical context to his argument and provide readers with a real-life figure whose actions and history likely influenced Virgil in his work. Both Aeneas and Augustus didn't show *clementia* to their enemies for strategic reasons.

16. E: While Sinon uses his tears and feigned sadness to move the Trojans to pity, perjury is used to describe him lying. Perjury actually means to willfully tell an untruth, so the definition fits. Aeneas is describing how masterfully skilled at lying Sinon was.

17. D: While the text does argue that Turnus was a major threat that Aeneas needed to eliminate, this was not explicitly said in this excerpt. The better answer would be D, because the author outlines this in his opening thesis: "While mercy is an ideal Aeneas is expected to live up to, his lack of mercy reflects necessary action in the war to fulfill his destiny and enact justice after the offences of Turnus."

18. B: Book 10 recounts the killing of Magus, paragraph 5.

19. D:. This is an example of a purpose question—*why* did the author write this? The article contains facts, definitions, and other objective information without telling a story or arguing an opinion. In this case, the purpose of the article is to inform the reader. The only answer choice that is related to giving information is answer Choice *D*: to define and describe.

20. A: A general definition followed by more specific examples. This organization question asks readers to analyze the structure of the essay. The topic of the essay is about spinoff technology; the first paragraph gives a general definition of the concept, while the following two paragraphs offer more detailed examples to help illustrate this idea.

21. C: They were looking for ways to add health benefits to food. This reading comprehension question can be answered based on the second paragraph—scientists were concerned about astronauts' nutrition and began researching useful nutritional supplements. A in particular is not true because it reverses the order of discovery (first NASA identified algae for astronaut use, and then it was further developed for use in baby food).

22. B: Related to the brain. This vocabulary question could be answered based on the reader's prior knowledge; but even for readers who have never encountered the word "neurological" before, the passage does provide context clues. The very next sentence talks about "this algae's potential to boost brain health," which is a paraphrase of "neurological benefits." From this context, readers should be able to infer that "neurological" is related to the brain.

23. D: To give an example of valuable space equipment. This purpose question requires readers to understand the relevance of the given detail. In this case, the author mentions "costly and crucial equipment" before mentioning space suit visors, which are given as an example of something that is very valuable. *A* is not correct because fashion is only related to sunglasses, not to NASA equipment. *B* can be eliminated because it is simply not mentioned in the passage. While *C* seems like it could be a true statement, it is also not relevant to what is being explained by the author.

24. C: It is difficult to make money from scientific research. The article gives several examples of how businesses have been able to capitalize on NASA research, so it is unlikely that the author would agree with this statement. Evidence for the other answer choices can be found in the article: *A*, the author mentions that "many consumers are unaware that products they are buying are based on NASA research"; *B* is a general definition of spinoff technology; and *D* is mentioned in the final paragraph.

25. B: It would have been a nice touch for the author to mention other products in addition to the ones they described. Choices A, *C*, and *D* relate to the topic but do not fit as closely with the purpose of the passage (to define and describe instances of spinoff technology) as does Choice *B*.

Situational Judgment

Presentation of Situational Judgment Questions

Situational judgment questions present hypothetical situations and ask the test taker to identify the most and least effective selections out of the multiple-choice answers listed. Most of the situations pertain to the personal and professional relationships between an officer and his/her subordinates or superiors. The format is similar for all situational judgment questions.

Purpose of Situational Judgment Questions

The situational judgment questions have been recently added to the AFOQT in an attempt to better predict how a person might react in different situations. The answers given are used to evaluate the test taker's behavioral tendencies in judgment, leadership, knowledge, and independent problem solving. It is advised that these questions be answered with the Air Force core values in mind: integrity first, service before self, and excellence in all we do.

Preparing and Studying for Situational Judgment Questions

The situational-judgment questions are not the typical knowledge-based questions found on most tests, so there is no material to study or memorize. These questions are behavior based and pertain to personality. When choosing answers in this section, think about what is professional and how to avoid involving superiors unless absolutely necessary. Officers are expected to be resourceful people with integrity, and they are expected to treat others with the same respect they are shown. Answers chosen in the situational judgment section should reflect this.

Practice Questions

Situation 1

You have an innovative plan for your unit that, in your opinion, will improve performance. Not everyone in the unit is of the same opinion, and some downright oppose your plan. Even though the plan has not been put in motion, someone has already written a letter of complaint and sent it to your superior.

What would you do?
    a. Don't worry about anyone else's opinion, and implement the plan.
    b. Ignore the letter of complaint, and push forward with the plan.
    c. Have a meeting with the unit, including the person who wrote the complaint to your superior, and explain to everyone again the chain-of-command and how it is to be used.
    d. Discipline the person who wrote the letter of complaint so that no one else in the unit will break the chain-of-command in the future.
    e. Give up your plan in the wake of opposition, and see what the unit would like to do.

1. Select the answer that contains the MOST EFFECTIVE way to respond to the situation.

2. Select the answer that contains the LEAST EFFECTIVE way to respond to the situation.

Situation 2

You have had a successful working relationship with an aide assigned to you. On a personal level, you dislike the assignee based on your opinion that they are arrogant and too critical of others. A senior officer is thinking of giving the aide a promotion, which would greatly benefit his/her future and put the aide on a fast track for future promotions.

What would you do?
    a. Attempt to dissuade the senior officer by sharing your personal feelings about the aide.
    b. You want the aide to just go away, so you give a recommendation for promotion.
    c. You do not want the aide to be rewarded, so you recommend that the senior officer give it to someone else.
    d. Other than expressing your opinion of the aide, you do not interfere with the selection process.
    e. List your complaints about the aide in an anonymous letter to the senior officer.

3. Select the answer that contains the MOST EFFECTIVE way to respond to the situation.

4. Select the answer that contains the LEAST EFFECTIVE way to respond to the situation.

Situation 3

A coworker, who is another officer in your division, has to give an important speech in a few days. The officer has spent a great deal of time and effort on the report, but is still nervous about presenting it. After being asked by the officer to look over the report, you find some items that you feel need to be changed. You discuss these items with the other officer, who disagrees with you. You are positive that the changes you identified need to be made.

What would you do?
    a. Mention the conversation to a senior officer prior to the speech as a way to make yourself look better, since you are right and the other officer wouldn't listen to you.
    b. Do everything you can to convince the officer to review the report and supporting information and make the changes you have recommended.
    c. Avoid going to the speech if at all possible.
    d. Attempt to get a senior officer involved to order that the report be changed.
    e. Do not say or do anything. You are not giving the speech.

5. Select the answer that contains the MOST EFFECTIVE way to respond to the situation.

6. Select the answer that contains the LEAST EFFECTIVE way to respond to the situation.

Situation 4

You have been teamed up with another officer on an important one-month assignment to draft a report. Unfortunately, early in the project your coworker has become ill and is required to be on leave. The illness keeps him/her out of the office much longer than expected. At the one-month mark on the report, your coworker is still ill and remains on leave. There is no way of knowing when your coworker will return to work and his/her expertise is needed to complete the assignment.

What would you do?
    a. Order a subordinate onto the project in an attempt to complete the report.
    b. To the best of your ability, put in as many hours as it takes to finish it yourself.
    c. Don't give any details; just ask for the deadline to be extended.
    d. Relay the situation to your superior and request help to finish the report.
    e. Wait indefinitely for the coworker to return without regard to the timeline for the report.

7. Select the answer that contains the MOST EFFECTIVE way to respond to the situation.

8. Select the answer that contains the LEAST EFFECTIVE way to respond to the situation.

Situation 5

After a long day at work, you are at home and you realize you forgot to sign documents that need to go on to another unit for completion. The documents cannot move forward without your signature. While the documents are not urgent in nature, your oversight will cause another officer to be delayed and have to stay at work later than usual.

What would you do?
    a. Go back to work and sign the papers.
    b. The documents are not urgent, so you wait until the next day to sign them.
    c. Show up to work early the next day to sign the documents, get them moving first thing in the morning, and hope the other officer won't have to stay late.
    d. Get a subordinate at your office to sign your name on the documents so they can move forward.
    e. Call the officer that this will impact and explain that the documents will be late in arriving.

9. Select the answer that contains the MOST EFFECTIVE way to respond to the situation.

10. Select the answer that contains the LEAST EFFECTIVE way to respond to the situation.

Situation 6

A week before you are about to be transferred to a new unit you receive a message from the officer in charge of that unit. The officer explains you are entering the unit at a critical time, as they are leading training exercises for highly skilled soldiers. The message goes on to indicate that you are expected to be a valuable contributor from the moment you arrive, with minimal assistance. However, your experience in this area is minimal.

What would you do?
    a. Send a courteous thank you message in return and attempt to study for the new position.
    b. Send no response to the email. You should have no problem taking on this new position.
    c. Discreetly ask one of the officers in the new unit if he/she will be able to train you upon arrival.
    d. You think you should remain with your current unit, so you request that your transfer be cancelled.
    e. Respond to the senior officer's message with a request for a meeting, where you can discuss transition into the new position.

11. Select the answer that contains the MOST EFFECTIVE way to respond to the situation.

12. Select the answer that contains the LEAST EFFECTIVE way to respond to the situation.

Situation 7

A coworker, who is another officer, has lied about his/her time off. The officer had requested leave for a week to visit an ailing family member. The request for leave was granted. Through social media, you learned the officer was at the beach on vacation, hundreds of miles away from the ailing family member he/she was supposedly visiting.

What would you do?
    a. Go see the commanding officer immediately to relay what you just discovered.
    b. Anonymously send the social media evidence of the officer's actions to the commanding officer.
    c. Since you now have a bargaining chip, you tell the officer you will keep this information to yourself in exchange for him taking on part of your weekly workload.
    d. Tell the officer if he/she does anything unethical like that again you will have no choice but to report it.
    e. You mind your own business and do nothing.

13. Select the answer that contains the MOST EFFECTIVE way to respond to the situation.

14. Select the answer that contains the LEAST EFFECTIVE way to respond to the situation.

Situation 8

After being in the same unit and performing the same job for two years, you are beginning to feel burned out. Even though you are successful in your current position, you wonder what other options may be available. You have been asking around to people in other units to gauge their experiences. Within a month the rumors in your unit have started that are you are looking for a transfer.

What would you do?
    a. Address the concerns that are brought up and refocus on your current position.
    b. Ask for a leave of absence so you can find a way to handle the situation.
    c. Send a formal request for transfer to your senior officer, acknowledging the truth of the rumors.
    d. Refocus on your position and ignore the rumors, even though they are true.
    e. Continue looking for a new unit to transfer to, but deny the rumors that are circulating.

15. Select the answer that contains the MOST EFFECTIVE way to respond to the situation.

16. Select the answer that contains the LEAST EFFECTIVE way to respond to the situation.

Situation 9

Your current workload has you extremely busy, but you are managing to meet your deadlines and are producing quality work. A senior officer has asked if you would perform an additional assignment in conjunction with the work you are performing. While you would like to impress the senior officer and take on the additional work, you are already pushing yourself with your current workload. If you took on the extra work, the quality of work on both assignments would suffer.

What would you do?
    a. Tell the senior officer that you would be glad to do the work, and then pass it on to a coworker to complete.
    b. Apologize to the senior officer, and say you are too busy and that you cannot do the extra assignment.
    c. Ask for a few days to think about it.
    d. You can't say no so you take the assignment; you will just have to find a way to complete the work as quickly as possible.
    e. Present an offer to pass the assignment to another qualified coworker, but inform the senior officer that unfortunately you are unable to complete the work yourself at this time.

17. Select the answer that contains the MOST EFFECTIVE way to respond to the situation.

18. Select the answer that contains the LEAST EFFECTIVE way to respond to the situation.

Situation 10

While assigned to a field office, you become aware that a coworker is extremely overworked with assignments being sent from other offices. The coworker's senior officers do not seem to notice that this person is overworked because your coworker does an excellent job, but they need to work extra hours to get the tasks completed.

What would you do?
    a. You do nothing. That situation has nothing to do with you.
    b. Sympathize with the coworker about his/her workload.
    c. Assist the coworker and help with his/her workload as much as possible.
    d. Request a meeting with the coworker's senior officer to inform the officer of the situation.
    e. Task one of your subordinates to assist this person in the workload.

19. Select the answer that contains the MOST EFFECTIVE way to respond to the situation.

20. Select the answer that contains the LEAST EFFECTIVE way to respond to the situation.

Situation 11

You are in attendance at a meeting where two officers get in a heated dispute over policy changes. It is considered common knowledge around work that these two officers do not like each other on a personal level, but no one is sure why. Unable to come to an agreement on the policy, they ask you to settle the disagreement.

What would you do?
    a. Resolve the dispute on the side of the officer that you favor.
    b. Resolve the dispute on the side of the officer who can benefit your career the most in the future.
    c. Put all personal feelings aside and choose what you believe is the best option.
    d. Point out the officers' blatant issues with each other as the reason they cannot agree, and then remove yourself from the situation.
    e. Disregard the request to settle the dispute on the policy; this is a good time to lecture these two on teamwork and cooperation in the military.

21. Select the answer that contains the MOST EFFECTIVE way to respond to the situation.

22. Select the answer that contains the LEAST EFFECTIVE way to respond to the situation.

Situation 12

You are working on reports for your senior officers with a coworker. The reports are used by the officers to track the training and readiness of soldiers for the most hazardous and difficult missions. You noticed your coworker appears to be manipulating these numbers, and they are not being entered correctly. If the soldiers are reported as having a higher amount of training than is required for these missions and then chosen, this could pose a huge risk to the missions and put lives in jeopardy.

What would you do?
    a. Do nothing yet, but monitor the coworker to see what is going on.
    b. Report this issue to your senior officer right away.
    c. Review your coworker's numbers and correct them yourself.
    d. Leave an anonymous note to your coworker to stop changing the numbers in the report and make sure what is turned in is accurate.
    e. Wait for coworker to finish assignment, and then you will have proof of what is going on.

23. Select the answer that contains the MOST EFFECTIVE way to respond to the situation.

24. Select the answer that contains the LEAST EFFECTIVE way to respond to the situation.

Situation 13

A senior officer asks you in private how you feel about your supervisor. Your supervisor reports to this senior officer. You feel the officer in question overall does a good job, but could do better in a certain aspect of his/her job.

What would you do?
    a. Express just that: They do a good job overall, but could use improvement in this one area.
    b. Refuse to answer the question.
    c. Give the supervisor a glowing review, without mentioning his/her weak area.
    d. Discuss the solutions to improving the area the officer is weak.
    e. Write a note that explains your thoughts about the officer.

25. Select the answer that contains the MOST EFFECTIVE way to respond to the situation.

26. Select the answer that contains the LEAST EFFECTIVE way to respond to the situation.

Situation 14

You are serving on a board of three officers interviewing three candidates for promotion. Candidate 1 is a known family friend of your commanding officer, but is the most impressive of the three candidates through the interview process. Candidate 2 seems to be another good choice for the position. Candidate 3 did not do well in the interview process and does not seem like a good choice for promotion at this point. The other two officers on the board have voted, one for each of the first two candidates. You have the deciding vote.

What would you do?
    a. You cast your vote for the second candidate, to avoid the appearance of favoritism.
    b. You remove yourself from the board so that you do not have to vote.
    c. You vote for Candidate 3, so you do not have to decide who gets the promotion.
    d. You vote for Candidate 1, because that candidate is most qualified.
    e. You refrain from the vote and ask for a new group of candidates.

27. Select the answer that contains the MOST EFFECTIVE way to respond to the situation.

28. Select the answer that contains the LEAST EFFECTIVE way to respond to the situation.

Situation 15

You are given an important assignment that involves working with an officer from a different unit. This officer appears to already have "one foot out the door," as retirement is near. The officer does not put much effort into the assignment, leaving you to do the bulk of the work.

What would you do?
    a. Explain your feelings to your new coworker. Point out that the situation is not fair to you and that the work is very important and should be shared equally.
    b. Put in a request for a new partner on the assignment.
    c. Say nothing and do all the work necessary to successfully complete the assignment.
    d. Just do the best you can with the realization the assignment will likely be unsuccessful due to lack of participation of your coworker.
    e. Inform your senior officer of the situation.

29. Select the answer that contains the MOST EFFECTIVE way to respond to the situation.

30. Select the answer that contains the LEAST EFFECTIVE way to respond to the situation.

Situation 16

You have had a feeling that one of your subordinates may have an ambitious agenda and be deliberately undermining your work. Other officers have discussed that this subordinate wants to take your job.

What would you do?
    a. Publicly attempt to humiliate the subordinate and reprimand him/her.
    b. Do nothing and the situation may just go away.
    c. Discuss the situation with the subordinate and explain that you expect his/her cooperation and support.
    d. Ask for another officer to step in and discuss the problem with your subordinate.
    e. File a report for insubordination to your senior officer.

31. Select the answer that contains the MOST EFFECTIVE way to respond to the situation.

32. Select the answer that contains the LEAST EFFECTIVE way to respond to the situation.

Situation 17

Recently it has come to your attention that office supplies are disappearing from the supply closet at a much faster rate than usual. There is no apparent reason that would account for the change in supply usage. Your gut is telling you that the officer that is last to leave the office may be taking items with him/her after everyone else has left. You do not have any evidence of your suspicion, but it does seem like things disappear on the shifts for which this officer is the last to leave.

What would you do?
    a. Report your suspicions to a senior officer.
    b. Secretly set up hidden cameras in an attempt to catch the thief.
    c. Discuss your suspicions with the officer you suspect and ask for an explanation.
    d. Discuss with fellow officers to see what they think is going on.
    e. Don't do anything.

33. Select the answer that contains the MOST EFFECTIVE way to respond to the situation.

34. Select the answer that contains the LEAST EFFECTIVE way to respond to the situation.

Situation 18

Rumors have been circulating that your base is going to be shut down due to budgetary restraints. You are in attendance at a meeting between local community leaders and senior officers from your unit. The community leaders are willing to lobby to keep the base open in return for the support of the military leadership in some local initiatives, specifically disaster-relief coordination efforts. A community leader asks your opinion on the matter being discussed.

What would you do?
    a. Answer the question honestly to the best of your ability, but explain you are not a senior officer.
    b. Tell the leader you are not a senior officer and cannot give your opinion.
    c. Defer the question to a senior officer without giving your opinion.
    d. Give a thorough answer even though you have little knowledge on this topic.
    e. Answer the question, but keep it positive; do not mention any possible negative result of what is being proposed.

35. Select the answer that contains the MOST EFFECTIVE way to respond to the situation.

36. Select the answer that contains the LEAST EFFECTIVE way to respond to the situation.

Situation 19

A subordinate in your unit has recently been showing signs of burnout and seems frustrated with his/her current position over the last month. You notice this coincides with a decline in the quality and quantity of his/her work. This negative attitude has been affecting the overall work environment with the fellow soldiers in the unit.

What would you do?
    a. Report the situation to your senior officer.
    b. You do nothing and hope the situation will improve on its own.
    c. Point out this behavior and bad performance in a meeting with the entire unit.
    d. Meet with the subordinate to discuss these issues, along with the effects on the unit, and present possible solutions.
    e. Reassign the subordinate to alleviate the problem in your unit.

37. Select the answer that contains the MOST EFFECTIVE way to respond to the situation.

38. Select the answer that contains the LEAST EFFECTIVE way to respond to the situation.

Situation 20

In your current position, one of your many responsibilities is to brief a small team of some activities that are confidential in nature. You have accidentally sent an email containing some of this confidential information to an officer that is not on this team, and who does not have the security clearance to have access to the information you sent.

What would you do?
  a. Immediately email this person and request they destroy the information you just sent. Then, immediately inform your supervisor of your mistake.
  b. Tell your supervisor what happened and let him/her handle it.
  c. You do nothing. Wait and see what happens.
  d. Ask your senior officer if they can request that the individual be cleared for a higher security level since they have been presented with the material.
  e. Send an email to the same person saying your email was hacked and to disregard any previous messages.

39. Select the answer that contains the MOST EFFECTIVE way to respond to the situation.

40. Select the answer that contains the LEAST EFFECTIVE way to respond to the situation.

Situation 21

Soldiers in your unit have been awaiting training at a nearby base. A request was made to be in the next training cycle, but soldiers from a different unit were chosen for the next block of training—even though they had not been waiting as long. You have no evidence, but you have a feeling your unit may not have been given the training block requested due to the training director disliking you on a personal level.

What would you do?
  a. Ask the director if your soldiers can attend the same training along with the other soldiers selected.
  b. Meet with the training director to determine the reason your soldiers were passed over, and emphasize the importance of this training to your unit.
  c. Do nothing; the decision has been made.
  d. Send a critical letter to the director and your senior officer over this perceived injustice.
  e. Discuss the situation with the other unit's senior officer to see if they would give up their training spots so your soldiers could have them.

41. Select the answer that contains the MOST EFFECTIVE way to respond to the situation.

42. Select the answer that contains the LEAST EFFECTIVE way to respond to the situation.

Situation 22

When you joined a new unit a couple of months ago, the leader of the unit was very helpful. You were given a great deal of training to carry out the duties and responsibilities of your new position. You are now feeling pretty confident in your abilities, but still have not been given the freedom to work your position independently.

What would you do?
   a. Tell the unit leader's supervisor that they need to back off and give you the leeway to do your job.
   b. Provide evidence and demonstrate your competence so the leader will leave you alone.
   c. Meet with the leader, thank him for all the assistance and guidance, and discuss that you feel ready to work more independently.
   d. Try to avoid the leader as much as possible and maybe the situation will correct itself.
   e. Request another officer be assigned to your unit so that the leader will need to refocus attention on someone else.

43. Select the answer that contains the MOST EFFECTIVE way to respond to the situation.

44. Select the answer that contains the LEAST EFFECTIVE way to respond to the situation.

Situation 23

Almost two months ago you were assigned to a new unit. In that brief amount of time you have identified numerous deficiencies in existing operations and have developed solutions for these problems. The majority of the people you have discussed these issues with agree with your proposed solutions. However, the senior officer believes the solutions are too risky and may cause more harm than good.

What would you do?
   a. Implement your proposed solutions, believing the senior officer will come around once he/she witnesses their success.
   b. Accept the senior officer's decision and work within the current structure without making your changes.
   c. Using the majority support of the unit, again confront the senior officer with your solutions.
   d. In detail, create a comprehensive report on the benefits of implementing your proposed solutions. Deliver your report and subsequently accept your senior officer's decision either way.
   e. Accept the senior officer's decision, then keep a log of the ways your solutions could have improved performance.

45. Select the answer that contains the MOST EFFECTIVE way to respond to the situation.

46. Select the answer that contains the LEAST EFFECTIVE way to respond to the situation.

Situation 24

You have always excelled in your work, and you received a promotion six months ago. Recent budget cuts have affected the quality of your work over the last few weeks. The budget cuts prevented you from having what you needed to perform your job efficiently and in the proper way. Your senior officer, however, is unaware of the budget effects and has expressed that you are the problem, your work is not up to par, and the performance drop is a result of poor management on your part.

What would you do?
 a. Ask for advice or ideas from other officers who are dealing with the same issues resulting from budget problems.
 b. Tell your senior officer the problem lies with your subordinates.
 c. Get a list of complaints from your senior officer.
 d. Ask for time off to get some perspective.
 e. Defend your position and remind the senior officer of the budget cuts.

47. Select the answer that contains the MOST EFFECTIVE way to respond to the situation.

48. Select the answer that contains the LEAST EFFECTIVE way to respond to the situation.

Situation 25

Supply and delivery logistics are maintained in a base computer program. While you are coordinating a long line of deliveries, the computer system crashes. You are advised by computer support the problem may take an hour or more to fix. The delivery drivers are already getting impatient.

What would you do?
 a. Request guidance from a senior officer.
 b. Ask the drivers if they have any other deliveries they could make in the meantime and return later.
 c. Try to avoid the drivers by going on a break.
 d. Ask for assistance in advising all drivers of the issue and the possible wait time, and accommodate them in whatever way you can.
 e. Receive the deliveries anyway.

49. Select the answer that contains the MOST EFFECTIVE way to respond to the situation.

50. Select the answer that contains the LEAST EFFECTIVE way to respond to the situation.

Answer Explanations

1. C: (Most effective) Having an open meeting with everyone would reemphasize the important of the chain-of-command and resolve problems at the lowest possible level.

2. E: (Least effective) Giving up your position because of opposition would demonstrate weakness as a leader and lead to similar actions in future decisions.

3. D: (Most effective) This is a case of *integrity first*. It is fine to voice your opinion to the aid, but better to refrain from interfering with the selection process based on personal feelings.

4. B or E: (Least effective) Giving a recommendation to make the aide go away would not uphold the core value of integrity. An honest opinion should always be given. The same could be said for an anonymous letter. Officers should always be forthright and honest when giving recommendations.

5. B: (Most effective) Part of being a good officer is to help peers. Try to point out what you would change in the speech and include why you would do it but letting the senior officer make the decision.

6. A: (Least effective) Never go to a superior with the intention of trying to make yourself look better by slandering a coworker. This is an integrity violation and will erode your credibility as an officer.

7. D: (Most effective) Situations come up in every unit that can impact the mission. In this situation, notify your supervisor immediately so they can get someone to replace the ill coworker and accomplish the mission.

8. B: (Least effective) Do not try to finish the project by yourself. Notify your supervisor immediately any time a situation arises that may impact completing the mission on time.

9. A: (Most effective) Be a professional and return to work. Sign the documents so that you are not causing another officer to work late due to your honest mistake.

10. D: (Least effective) Having a subordinate forge the documents puts your integrity and that of the subordinate at risk. Do not let a minor mistake like forgetting to sign a piece of paper ruin your credibility.

11. E: (Most effective) A response to the new commander's email would be the best solution to this scenario. Let him know that you are excited to take the new position and that you would like to set up a date and time to discuss the new role. This will help ensure a smooth transition.

12. B: (Least effective) Always take the opportunity to respond to an email from your new commander. It is the professional thing to do and will allow time to discuss what is expected of the new position, answer any questions, and learn how to excel.

13. D: (Most effective) This is an opportunity to teach, coach, and mentor a fellow officer by discussing the Air Force core values. By talking to the coworker and not telling his/her superior officer, you offer this person a chance to grow from the mistake without hurting his/her career.

14. C: (Least effective) Resorting to blackmail would make you just as guilty as your peer and would put your integrity on the line.

15. C: (Most effective) It is normal to reach a plateau in assignments. Let your senior officer know, and express that you are looking for a more challenging assignment to further your career and benefit the Air Force.

16. E: (Least effective) Remember, integrity first. Be honest in everything you do and no one can question your integrity.

17. E: (Most effective) Be honest with the officer and let him/her know that you are already dealing with a maximum workload. In addition, you have offered a solution to the problem by offering to distribute the work to another qualified coworker.

18. D: (Least effective) Taking on additional work without sufficient time will cause the quality of both projects to diminish.

19. D: (Most effective) Inform the senior officer of the situation and see if the projects can be redistributed to help alleviate stress for coworkers that are overwhelmed.

20. A: (Least effective) You were attentive to notice the situation; this is a good time to put service before self and offer a solution to the problem.

21. C: (Most effective) They asked you to resolve the dispute, so be the professional and make a decision.

22. E: (Least effective) Giving a lecture to both officers that asked you to settle the dispute would probably turn both of them against you. They must value your opinion, or they would not have asked for your assistance.

23. B: (Most effective) Safety issues need to be addressed immediately. It is your duty as an officer to notify the senior officer in charge if a coworker is manipulating numbers that could lead to an accident or incident.

24. A: (Least effective) It is your responsibility to speak up in this scenario. Again, integrity first - anyone can prevent an accident.

25. A: (Most effective) If the senior officer asks the question, they want an answer. Be honest, and offer a candid assessment in the area in which he/she could improve.

26. B: (Least effective) Again, if a senior officer asks the question, he/she is looking for an answer. Refusing makes you and your supervisor look bad.

27. D: (Most effective) Make the correct decision and vote for the most qualified candidate.

28. C: (Least effective) By voting for Candidate 3, you are not being honest. Remember the honest decision is not always going to be the easiest. If you are always honest, no one will ever question your integrity.

29. A: (Most effective) Let your new coworker know that you want to do your best on this project, you value his/her help, and you think the work should be shared equally. In addition, offer congratulations on the coworker's upcoming retirement and encourage him/her to finish strong.

30. D: (Least effective) Do not have the frame of mind that the project is going to be mediocre or it will. Talk to your new coworker and come up with a plan to share the workload and develop a quality product.

31. C: (Most effective) Talk with the subordinate and let him/her know what you have heard and that you need his/her support in accomplishing the unit's mission.

32. B: (Least effective) Something has to be done in this scenario. If not, the situation is going to get worse.

33. C: (Most effective) The best action to take in this scenario would be to question the last officer to leave the supply room. This would allow him/her to explain the situation without directly accusing him/her of stealing, and it would be an initial step in the investigative process.

34. E: (Least effective) If no action is taken, supplies are going to keep disappearing, and the situation is not going to get any better.

35. A: (Most effective) Give an honest opinion on the subject, and explain you are not a subject-matter expert. In addition, refer to media and to the base public affairs office for further information.

36. B: (Least effective) Not answering the question could portray a negative opinion of the officer.

37. D: (Most effective) Meet with the unit and discuss the issue that has been presented. Offer a solution to the problem, stay positive, and make sure there is an opportunity for subordinates to take a break.

38. A: (Least effective) Always try and solve the problem before going to senior leadership. This would create distrust among subordinates and show senior officers a lack of leadership and inability to handle simple unit challenges.

39. A: (Most effective) Be honest and admit your mistake. The person receiving the email will be more than willing to delete the material. Your supervisor will appreciate the honesty and inform the chain-of-command.

40. E: (Least effective) Do not lie about the situation. All classified email chains are monitored, and covering up this mistake could lead to revocation of a security clearance.

41. B: (Most effective) Meeting with the training director may open up an opportunity for training in the near future. It also shows the commanding officer cares about the unit and people.

42. D: (Least effective) Sending out letters would be perceived as a false accusation, damage your reputation, and could have an effect on future requests for training.

43. C: (Most effective) The leader may not have realized they were creating this environment. Meeting with the superior will clear the air, and it should afford an opportunity to work more independently.

44. A: (Least effective) Telling the supervisor to back off would create animosity and make the situation worse.

45. D: (Most effective) Ultimately, the boss has the final decision. A well thought out plan with actions and contingencies may sway his/her decision.

46. A: (Least effective) This would be insubordination no matter how the plan worked out. Either way, the boss would feel disrespected.

47. A: (Most effective) Budget cuts will affect everyone in the unit. Talking to peers can offer solutions that may not have been previously discovered.

48. B: (Least effective) Do not blame subordinates. This will erode trust in the unit.

49. D: (Most effective) Keeping the drivers informed of the delay will help with them understand the situation. Accommodating them will help build rapport for future deliveries.

50. C: (Least effective) This would frustrate the drivers even more and may have an effect on future deliveries.

Self-Description Inventory

The self-description inventory is a personality test provided in the last section of the AFOQT. The self-description inventory is not included in the final score, so no one answer is better than another. Since these questions are helpful in assessing your personal characteristics, answer them as best you can and don't spend much time analyzing them. The purpose is to find an appropriate career match by comparing your answers to others who hold Air Force positions.

Physical Science

Measurements

Scientific fields typically use the International System of Units (SI) for measurements. The International System of Units is also known as the metric system, and is based on the number 10. Although science uses SI for measurements, the United States uses the English system. Unlike the English system, the SI base unit for length is meter and the base unit for mass is kilogram. (The corresponding units in the English system are foot and pound, respectively.) Other less commonly used SI base units include ampere for electric current, Kelvin for thermodynamic temperature, mole for an amount of a substance, and candela for luminous intensity. To illustrate the amount of the base units, prefixes are used in front of the base units; for example, kilo in front of meter (kilometer) means 1,000 meters.

Matter

Matter is anything that has mass and volume, and mass is the amount of matter in an object. Most people believe that mass and weight are the same thing, but mass is not altered by gravity, while weight is the force of gravity on an object. In other words, mass will not be different in places with different gravities, but weight will change based on gravity differences.

Matter can be sorted into one of three phases: solids, liquids, and gases. In solids, particles are close together and can vibrate but cannot move apart because of their strong attractions for each other. Solids also have a definite shape and volume. Particles in liquids, on the other hand, are farther apart and can slide past one another. Liquids also have a definite volume, but no definite shape; they take on the shape of their container. Particles are even farther apart in gases and are free to move anywhere in a container. Gases also have no definite volume or shape.

Phases of matter change in different ways, including melting, freezing, vaporization, and condensation. As an object is heated, it turns from a solid to a liquid in a process called *melting*. Conversely, as it cools, it turns from a liquid to a solid when it *freezes*. A substance **vaporizes**, or *evaporates*, when it is heated to become a gas, and a substance *condenses* when it is in a gaseous state and is cooled, becoming a liquid. A substance changes from a solid to a gas through *sublimation*.

Motion and Forces

Motion and forces are a critical component of physical science but speed, velocity, and acceleration often get confused. The speed of an object is the rate at which an object moves, while velocity is a speed with a given direction. Finally, acceleration is the rate of change in velocity. For example, the pull of Earth's gravity creates a form of acceleration (gravitational acceleration); it is the acceleration of an object toward Earth.

Velocity is also related to momentum. Momentum depends on the mass and velocity of an object and is given by the following equation:

Momentum = mass x velocity

The Law of Conservation of Momentum states that the total momentum of a group of objects stays the same unless outside forces act on the objects; in other words, no momentum is lost, it is just transferred from one object to another.

Acceleration is also related to force. A force causes a change in the speed or direction of an object and is given by the following equation of Newton's Second Law of motion:

Force = mass x acceleration

More than one force can act on an object at one time, and the object will move in the direction of the greater force. Newton's Third Law of motion states that forces come in pairs so that for every action, there is an equal and opposite reaction.

Friction can influence the velocity or acceleration of an object. Friction acts in the opposite direction of motion and will cause a moving object to slow down and eventually stop. There are four types of friction: static, sliding, rolling, and fluid friction. Static friction occurs between stationary objects, while sliding friction occurs when solid objects slide over each other. Rolling friction happens when a solid object rolls over another solid object, and fluid friction is friction when an object moves through a fluid or through fluid layers (gas or liquid). This includes the air resistance on an object.

Friction is also related to Newton's First Law of motion. It states that an object at rest stays at rest and an object in motion stays in motion unless acted on by an outside unbalanced force—like friction. Newton's First Law is also called the Law of Inertia, and inertia is the tendency of an object to resist a change in its motion.

Energy Work and Power

Force is also related to work: Work is defined as the force required to move an object a certain distance. To do work, the direction of the applied force must be the same as the direction of the motion. Work is given in units of N*m, also known as the joule (J), and by the following equation:

Work = force x distance moved

The rate of which work is being done is known as power and is provided by the following equation:

Power = work/change in time

Power is energy divided by time. The unit for power is known as a watt (W), which is equal to one joule per second.

The ability to do work is known as energy (measured in joules). Objects can gain energy when work is being done to them. Energy can be classified as kinetic or potential energy. Kinetic energy is the energy of motion, while potential energy is stored energy. According to the Law of Conservation of Energy, energy can neither be created nor destroyed.

The different forms of energy are mechanical, electromagnetic, nuclear, chemical, and heat. Mechanical energy is the energy associated with motion, while electromagnetic energy is the energy associated with moving electric charges. Nuclear energy is generated by splitting uranium atoms, a process known as fission, and chemical energy is energy that is released through chemical reactions. Thermal (or heat) energy is the energy from the internal motion of atoms, and it moves from warmer objects to cooler objects.

Heat can be transferred in three ways: conduction, convection, and radiation. Conduction is heat energy transferred from one substance to another or through a substance by direct contact between molecules. Conduction can take places in solids, liquids, and gases. Objects that transfer heat more efficiently are good conductors of heat, while objects that do no transfer heat efficiently are called insulators. Convection is heat energy transferred through gases and liquids by convection current, while radiation is heat energy transferred through empty space and can take place in gases and liquids.

Waves

Waves are periodic disturbances in a gas, liquid, or solid that are created as energy is transmitted. Waves do not carry matter; they transfer energy. There are three different forms of waves: compression, transverse, and surface waves. Transverse waves are waves in which particles of the medium move in a direction perpendicular to the direction waves move, and surface waves are waves in which the particles of the medium go through circular motions. Compression, or longitudinal, waves are waves in which the particles of the medium move in a direction parallel to the direction the waves move. When longitudinal waves are close together, it is known as compression. Rarefaction, on the other hand, occurs when the particles of a longitudinal wave are far apart.

Each part of a wave has a different name and is used in different calculations. The distance between one point on a wave and the exact same place on the next wave is the wavelength, while the period is the time it takes two crests or compressions to pass a fixed point. The three parts of a transverse wave are the crest, the trough, and amplitude. The crest is the highest point and the trough is the lowest point of a transverse wave, while the amplitude is the height of each of them.

The types of ways are as follows: electromagnetic waves, mechanical waves, sound waves, and water waves, and recent experiments have also proven the existence of gravitational waves. The gravitational wave requires no medium (or ether) in which to travel and its effects and behaviors are still being studied. Electromagnetic waves can transmit energy through a vacuum, while mechanical waves cannot; they must have a medium to transport the waves. As expected, sound waves travel through air and water waves travel through water.

The principles of how waves bend are used in many different fields and applications. Refraction and reflection are often confused with one another. Refraction is the term for when a wave bends (such as when the medium it is traveling through changes). An example of refraction is the bending of light as it passes through a prism or sunlight passing through raindrops creating a rainbow. However, reflection is when a wave bounces off of a surface (like light bouncing off of a mirror or sound bouncing off of canyon walls in an echo). Similar to refraction, diffraction is when a wave bends around an object (such as when the medium it is traveling through runs into a barrier). A good example of diffraction is seeing water waves bending around a jetty or coming through the opening in a harbor. Finally, interference is when two waves collide and either create a larger wave or negate each other. Dropping two stones, side by side, into the water is a good example of interference. A real world application of this phenomenon is active noise cancelling headphones, which send out sound waves at certain wave lengths that interfere with incoming sound waves in order to 'cancel' them out.

The Atom, Periodic Table, and Radioactivity

Atoms form the basis of matter, and cannot be separated by physical or chemical means; in fact, all matter is made of atoms. An element is a pure substance composed completely of one type of atom; an example of an element is pure oxygen. The three parts of the atom are protons (positively charged), neutrons (neutral with no charge), and electrons (negatively charged). The electrons move freely in the electron cloud of an atom, while the protons and neutrons reside in the atomic nucleus. The nucleus of an atom is positively charged and the electron cloud is negatively charged. Protons and neutrons both have a mass of approximately 1 atomic mass unit, while electrons have an atomic mass unit of 0.0006 atomic mass units.

The number of protons in the nucleus of an atom is the atomic number. In a neutral atom, the number of protons equals the number of electrons. The atomic mass of an element is the number of protons plus the number of neutrons. To calculate the number of neutrons, use the following equation:

Neutrons = atomic mass - atomic number

The periodic table is a way of organizing known elements based on their atomic numbers (number of protons), properties, and configurations. Isotopes of an element have the same number of protons, but different numbers of neutrons. There can be many isotopes of the same element. In heavier elements (generally higher than number 83 on the periodic table), the strength binding the nucleus is weak and unstable; these elements are considered radioactive. This weak binding allows the nucleus to emit particles and energy through radioactive decay. Once enough radioactive emissions have occurred, the nucleus then becomes stable, forming an isotope.

A compound is the chemical bonding of two or more elements. A good example of a compound is water (H_2O). However, a compound is different from a mixture. A mixture is a combination of two or more pure substances that are not chemically combined; therefore, it is possible to physically separate a mixture. There are four types of mixtures: homogeneous mixtures, heterogeneous mixtures, colloids, and suspensions. A homogeneous mixture is comprised of two or more substances spread evenly without settling the same throughout, while heterogeneous mixtures are comprised of different parts that are distinguished easily. A colloid is a heterogeneous mixture that never settles, while suspensions contain a liquid with visible particles that settle out when it stands.

Electricity

Attraction occurs between particles that have opposite charges and repulsion occurs between particles that have the same charge; this force of attraction and repulsion is known as magnetism. Objects can develop electric charges when their atoms gain or lose electrons. Conductors, like metals, allow electrons to move through them easily. Insulators, like plastic, rubber, wood, or glass, do not allow electrons to move through them easily.

An electric current is a flow of electric charge. When a charge gets rearranged, this is known as induction. Current (I) is the amount of charge that passes a given point per unit of time and is measured in amperes or amps (A). In order to have a current, there must be a potential difference and a complete circuit.

A potential difference is the difference in potential between two places measured in volts (V), and a circuit is a closed path through which electrons can flow. Every circuit has a resistance level, measured in ohms; resistance is the opposition to the flow of electric charge. The amount of current that can flow through a circuit depends on voltage and how the wire resists the flow of electricity. Ohm's law gives us the relationship between voltage, current, and resistance. Ohm's Law is provided in the equation below:

Voltage = current x resistance

In electricity, electrical energy flows from objects with greater potential energy to objects with less potential energy. Batteries produce electricity by converting chemical energy into electrical energy. However, what about static electricity? Static electricity is the build-up of electric charges on an object, and the loss of static electricity is known as electric discharge. This build-up of electrical charges happens through the movement and/or rearrangement of electrons.

Practice Questions

1. The base unit measurement for mass in the International System of Units (SI) is:
   a. Meter
   b. Kelvin
   c. Kilogram
   d. Mole
   e. Pound

2. The change of a liquid to gas is known as:
   a. Vaporization
   b. Condensation
   c. Freezing
   d. Sublimation
   e. Heating

3. What is the definition of acceleration?
   a. The rate at which an object moves
   b. The rate of change in velocity
   c. Speed in a given direction
   d. The velocity of an object multiplied by its mass
   e. The rate of change in velocity of an object toward Earth

4. What is NOT a type of friction?
   a. Static
   b. Rolling
   c. Fluid
   d. Sliding
   e. Potential

5. What is the term for when a force moves an object over a distance?
   a. Work
   b. Power
   c. Energy
   d. Waves
   e. Force

6. What is the definition of radiation?
   a. Heat energy transferred between substances by direct contact between molecules
   b. Heat energy transferred through empty space
   c. When the particles of a longitudinal wave are close together
   d. Heat energy transferred through gases and liquids by convection currents
   e. Waves in which the particles of the medium go through circular motions

7. What is the function of a wave?
    a. To carry matter
    b. To transfer energy
    c. To do work
    d. To slow down matter
    e. To attract particles

8. Which is NOT a type of wave?
    a. Compression
    b. Transverse
    c. Electromagnetic
    d. Mechanical
    e. Atomic

9. What is the term for when a wave bends?
    a. Refraction
    b. Diffraction
    c. Reflection
    d. Interference
    e. Convection

10. What is the definition of a compound?
    a. A combination of two or more pure substances that are not chemically combined
    b. A substance made of two or more elements that are joined by chemical bonds
    c. A pure substance that cannot be separated by physical or chemical means
    d. A heterogeneous mixture
    e. A homogeneous mixture

11. What would H_2O be an example of?
    a. An element
    b. A mixture
    c. A colloid
    d. A compound
    e. An isotope

12. Which of the following reside in the nucleus of an atom?
    a. Protons
    b. Neutrons
    c. Electrons
    d. Both A and B
    e. Both A and C

13. The atomic number of oxygen is 8. How many protons are in oxygen?
    a. 8
    b. 32
    c. 16
    d. 14
    e. 22

14. The atomic mass of oxygen is 16. Using the same atomic number listed in question 13, calculate the number of neutrons in oxygen.
    a. 16
    b. 12
    c. 24
    d. 6
    e. 8

15. Which of the following materials is a conductor?
    a. Metal
    b. Plastic
    c. Rubber
    d. Wood
    e. Glass

16. What is the term for the force of attraction or repulsion between two objects or materials?
    a. Static electricity
    b. Electric discharge
    c. Magnetism
    d. Electric current
    e. Resistance

17. What is the unit of measurement (International System of Units) for current?
    a. Volts
    b. Amps
    c. Ohms
    d. Joules
    e. Watts

18. How does electrical energy flow?
    a. From objects with less potential energy to objects with greater potential energy
    b. Between objects with no energy
    c. From objects with greater potential energy to objects with less potential energy
    d. In an open path
    e. Between objects with equal potential energy

19. What does current NOT depend on?
    a. Voltage
    b. Resistance
    c. The wire
    d. The circuit
    e. Magnetism

20. What is the term for the highest point of a transverse wave?
    a. Amplitude
    b. Trough
    c. Crest
    d. Compression
    e. Wavelength

Answer Explanations

1. C: Kilogram is the base unit for mass in the International System of Units (SI). Meter is the base unit for length, Kelvin is the base unit for temperature, and mole is the base unit for an amount of a substance. Pound is the base unit for weight in the English system.

2. A: The change of a substance from a liquid to gas is called vaporization. Condensation is the change of a substance from a gas to a liquid, and freezing is the change of a substance from a liquid to a solid. Sublimation is the change of a solid to a gas, and heating is just the rise in temperature of a substance.

3. B: Acceleration is the rate of change in velocity. Speed is the rate at which an object moves, velocity is speed in a given direction, momentum is the velocity of an object multiplied by its mass, and gravity is the rate of change in velocity of an object toward Earth.

4. E: The four types of friction are static, sliding, rolling, and fluid friction. Potential friction is not a type of friction, although potential energy does exist.

5. A: Work happens when a force moves an object over a distance and is given by the following equation: Work = force x distance moved. Power is the rate at which work is being done, energy is the ability to do work, waves are a periodic disturbance in matter as energy is transmitted, and force is an object's mass multiplied by its acceleration.

6. B: Radiation is heat energy transferred through empty space and can occur in gases and liquids. Conduction is heat energy transferred between substances or within a substance by direct contact between molecules, compression is when the particles of a longitudinal wave are close together, convection is heat energy transferred through gases and liquids by convection currents, and surface waves are waves in which the particles of the medium go through circular motions.

7. B: Waves are periodic disturbances in a gas, liquid, or solid as energy is transmitted. Waves don't carry matter; they transfer energy.

8. E: Compression waves are waves in which the particles of the medium move in a direction parallel to the direction the waves move. Transverse waves are waves in which particles of the medium move in a direction perpendicular to the direction waves move. Electromagnetic waves can transmit energy through a vacuum. Mechanical waves cannot transmit energy through a vacuum; they must have a medium to transport the waves.

9. A: The definition of refraction is when a wave bends (such as when the medium it is traveling through changes). Diffraction is when a wave bends around an object (such as when the medium it is traveling through runs into a barrier). Reflection is when a wave bounces off of a surface, and interference is when a wave bounces off of a surface. Convection is heat energy transferred through gases and liquids by convection currents.

10. B: A compound is a substance made of two or more elements that are joined by chemical bonds. A mixture is a combination of two or more pure substances that are not chemically combined. An element is a pure substance that cannot be separated by physical or chemical means. (A compound could be separated by physical or chemical means.)

11. D: H_2O is an example of a compound because the hydrogen and oxygen atoms are held together by chemical bonds. The individual hydrogen and oxygen atoms themselves would be considered elements. H_2O would only be considered a mixture if the elements were not chemically combined. A colloid is another type of mixture: a heterogeneous mixture that never settles. An isotope is an element with a different number of neutrons.

12. D: Protons and neutrons both are in the atomic nucleus, while electrons move freely in the electron cloud of an atom. Therefore, the nucleus of an atom is positively charged and the electron cloud is negatively charged.

13. A: The atomic number of an element is also the number of protons in that element.

14. E: To calculate the number of neutrons in oxygen, subtract the atomic number from the atomic mass. The atomic mass of an element is the number of protons plus the number of neutrons.

15. A: Metal is a conductor of electricity, while plastic, rubber, wood, and glass are all insulators. Conductors allow electrons to move through them easily, while insulators do not allow electrons to move through them easily.

16. C: Magnetism is the force of attraction and repulsion between two objects or materials.

17. B: Current is the amount of charge that passes a given point per unit of time and is measured in amperes or amps.

18. C: Electricity moves from objects with greater potential energy to objects with less potential energy.

19. E: Current does not depend on magnetism, but depends on voltage, the resistance of the wire, and the circuit.

20. C: The crest is the highest point of a transverse wave. The trough is the lowest point of a transverse wave, and amplitude is how far the medium moves from a state of rest. Compression is when the particles of a longitudinal wave are close together. Wavelength is the distance between one point on a wave and the exact same place on the next wave.

Table Reading

This section of the test measures whether you can read a table accurately. The table below shows X- and Y-values in a grid format. The numbers on the horizontal, or top, part of the table are the X-values, and the numbers on the vertical, or side, part of the table are the Y-values. In other words, the X-values correspond to columns, and the Y-values correspond to rows. Each question will provide you with two coordinates, an X and a Y, and you must quickly interpret the table to determine the correct value. Each question will have five possible answers, and you should choose the correct one.

Using the example table below, here are some practice questions and explanations to better help you understand how to use these tables.

	-3	-2	-1	0	+1	+2	+3
+3	14	15	17	19	20	21	22
+2	15	17	19	21	22	23	24
+1	16	18	20	22	24	25	26
0	18	19	21	23	25	26	28
-1	20	22	23	25	27	28	30
-2	21	23	24	26	28	29	31
-3	22	24	25	27	29	30	32

Example Problem 1

X	Y		A	B	C	D	E
0	+1		22	25	20	19	16

The answer to this example question would be A, 22. To answer this problem, first go to the X-axis and find the 0 column. Then follow the 0 column down to the +1 row on the Y-axis. The number at that point is 22. Some corresponding coordinates for the incorrect answers in this example would be:

B = 25: +1, 0

C = 20: +1, +3

D = 19: 0, +3

E = 16: -3, +1

What are some helpful tips for answering these questions correctly?

- Take your time. The easiest way to make mistakes in this section is assuming that the questions are easy and subsequently making simple mistakes.

- Make sure to correctly read the X and Y headings. It is easy to select the second column when you have an X-value of 2, but that wouldn't be the right column.

- Start with the X coordinate and stay within that selected column. Do not mistakenly travel to another column when you are selecting the Y-value.

- After you have the X column selected, go down to the corresponding Y-value row. Remember, don't change columns!

- Use your fingers or a piece of paper to mark the columns and rows as it helps you keep track of where you are and not jump to a neighboring column or row.

- Practice these types of questions until you are comfortable answering them correctly and within a certain window of time. On test day, take the same amount of time as you had been with the practice questions.

Practice Questions

The next five questions are based on the following table.

	-3	-2	-1	0	1	2	3
-3	20	21	24	27	23	26	25
-2	21	22	29	32	31	30	26
-1	23	25	26	27	24	21	20
0	25	26	30	31	32	29	22
1	31	28	29	22	20	24	27
2	28	33	20	30	21	23	25
3	30	28	26	24	22	20	32

1. (-3, 3)
   a. 30
   b. 20
   c. 32
   d. 23
   e. 24

2. (0, -2)
   a. 30
   b. 26
   c. 32
   d. 21
   e. 29

3. (+1, 0)
   a. 22
   b. 30
   c. 24
   d. 27
   e. 32

4. (-2, -3)
   a. 23
   b. 21
   c. 33
   d. 26
   e. 20

5. (-1, 0)
   a. 22
   b. 27
   c. 24
   d. 30
   e. 23

The next five questions are based on the following table.

	-3	-2	-1	0	1	2	3
-3	10	11	13	15	18	17	19
-2	17	20	19	16	14	12	10
-1	18	19	17	20	13	11	16
0	13	22	18	14	12	10	11
1	11	19	20	16	15	14	18
2	19	23	22	12	17	15	20
3	14	15	12	18	11	22	21

6. (3, 3)
   a. 10
   b. 21
   c. 16
   d. 12
   e. 19

7. (-2, 1)
   a. 14
   b. 11
   c. 20
   d. 17
   e. 19

8. (0, 0)
   a. 14
   b. 15
   c. 13
   d. 10
   e. 12

9. (1, -2)
   a. 19
   b. 17
   c. 22
   d. 14
   e. 11

10. (-1, 0)
    a. 20
    b. 12
    c. 15
    d. 13
    e. 18

The next five questions are based on the following table.

	-3	-2	-1	0	1	2	3
-3	30	31	32	33	34	35	36
-2	33	34	35	36	37	38	39
-1	34	40	41	39	38	37	36
0	35	33	31	32	30	40	41
1	31	35	37	33	39	41	43
2	37	36	33	34	35	39	38
3	32	30	31	35	36	34	31

11. (2, -2)
   a. 34
   b. 36
   c. 39
   d. 35
   e. 38

12. (1, -3)
   a. 31
   b. 38
   c. 34
   d. 33
   e. 36

13. (3, 2)
   a. 38
   b. 34
   c. 37
   d. 39
   e. 33

14. (0, -1)
   a. 39
   b. 31
   c. 33
   d. 32
   e. 34

15. (-2, -1)
   a. 41
   b. 40
   c. 35
   d. 37
   e. 31

The next five questions are based on the following table.

	-3	-2	-1	0	1	2	3
-3	50	51	52	53	54	55	56
-2	53	55	56	57	58	59	52
-1	54	60	57	58	52	61	53
0	55	53	58	59	60	52	54
1	56	59	54	60	51	53	55
2	57	54	55	61	59	57	56
3	51	52	53	54	55	56	57

16. (-3, 2)
    a. 55
    b. 52
    c. 53
    d. 57
    e. 56

17. (-2, 0)
    a. 57
    b. 52
    c. 61
    d. 53
    e. 51

18. (1, 1)
    a. 51
    b. 57
    c. 52
    d. 54
    e. 55

19. (2, -1)
    a. 56
    b. 60
    c. 61
    d. 53
    e. 59

20. (-1, 3)
    a. 55
    b. 53
    c. 52
    d. 54
    e. 57

The next five questions are based on the following table.

	-3	-2	-1	0	1	2	3
-3	40	41	42	43	44	45	46
-2	42	44	43	54	47	46	45
-1	44	46	45	52	53	48	43
0	46	48	47	50	49	44	51
1	48	50	49	48	51	52	47
2	50	52	51	46	47	42	49
3	52	54	53	44	45	50	41

21. (0, 2)
  a. 46
  b. 44
  c. 54
  d. 48
  e. 52

22. (3, -2)
  a. 54
  b. 50
  c. 45
  d. 49
  e. 42

23. (-1, 1)
  a. 53
  b. 45
  c. 51
  d. 49
  e. 42

24. (2, 3)
  a. 49
  b. 54
  c. 41
  d. 45
  e. 50

25. (-2, 1)
  a. 47
  b. 50
  c. 48
  d. 46
  e. 52

The next five questions are based on the following table.

	-3	-2	-1	0	1	2	3
-3	5	6	7	8	9	10	11
-2	6	7	8	9	10	11	12
-1	8	9	10	11	12	13	14
0	10	11	12	13	14	15	16
1	12	13	14	15	16	17	6
2	14	15	16	17	6	5	8
3	16	17	6	5	8	7	10

26. (3, 0)
   a. 5
   b. 10
   c. 8
   d. 11
   e. 16

27. (1, 2)
   a. 17
   b. 6
   c. 16
   d. 10
   e. 8

28. (-1, -1)
   a. 16
   b. 14
   c. 10
   d. 12
   e. 7

29. (-3, -2)
   a. 7
   b. 12
   c. 6
   d. 14
   e. 8

30. (3, -1)
   a. 14
   b. 7
   c. 6
   d. 12
   e. 8

The next five questions are based on the following table.

	-3	-2	-1	0	1	2	3
-3	11	12	13	14	15	16	17
-2	12	13	14	15	16	17	18
-1	14	15	16	17	18	19	20
0	16	17	18	19	20	21	22
1	18	19	20	21	22	21	12
2	20	21	22	11	12	13	14
3	22	11	12	13	14	15	16

31. (-3, -1)
    a. 14
    b. 13
    c. 20
    d. 18
    e. 12

32. (0, 1)
    a. 20
    b. 17
    c. 21
    d. 18
    e. 14

33. (2, 1)
    a. 12
    b. 19
    c. 17
    d. 15
    e. 11

34. (3, -3)
    a. 22
    b. 17
    c. 16
    d. 11
    e. 20

35. (-1, 2)
    a. 19
    b. 16
    c. 14
    d. 22
    e. 12

The next five questions are based on the following table.

	-3	-2	-1	0	1	2	3
-3	20	21	22	23	24	25	26
-2	21	22	23	24	25	26	27
-1	23	24	25	26	27	28	29
0	25	26	27	28	29	30	31
1	27	28	29	30	31	20	21
2	29	30	31	20	21	22	23
3	31	20	21	22	23	24	25

36. (2, 2)
    a. 30
    b. 22
    c. 26
    d. 21
    e. 20

37. (1, -3)
    a. 27
    b. 23
    c. 24
    d. 29
    e. 22

38. (1, -1)
    a. 31
    b. 29
    c. 25
    d. 27
    e. 24

39. (2, -2)
    a. 26
    b. 30
    c. 22
    d. 20
    e. 21

40. (0, 3)
    a. 31
    b. 22
    c. 23
    d. 25
    e. 26

Answer Explanations

1. A: Select -3 on the horizontal X axis of the table and move down to +3 on the vertical Y axis. This number is 30. (-3, -3) is 20, (3, 3) is 32, (1, -3) is 23, and (-1, -3) is 24.

2. C: The X axis is 0, while the Y axis is -2; this number is 32. (0, 2) is 30, (-2, 0) is 26, (-2, -3) is 21, and (2, 0) is 29.

3. E: The X axis is +1, while the Y axis is 0; this number is 32. (0, 1) is 22, (-1, 0) is 30, (-1, -3) is 24, and (0, -1) is 27.

4. B: The X value is -2 and the Y value is -3; this number is 21. (-3, -1) is 23, (-2, -2) is 33, (2, -3) is 26, and (3, -1) is 20.

5. D: The X value is -1 and the Y value is 0; this number is 30. (0, 1) is 22, (0, -1) is 27, (-1, -3) is 24, and (-3, -1) is 23.

6. B: The X value is 3 and the Y value is 3; this number is 21. (-3, -3) is 10, (3, -1) is 16, (-1, 3) is 12, and (3, -3) is 19.

7. E: The X value is -2 and the Y value is 1; this number is 19. (1, -2) is 14, (2, -1) is 11, (-2,-2) is 20, and (-1, -1) is 17.

8. A: The X value is 0 and the Y value is 0; this number is 14. (0, -3) is 15, (-3, 0) is 13, (-3, -3) is 10, and (1, 0) is 12.

9. D: The X value is 1 and the Y value is -2; this number is 14. (-2, 1) is 19, (1, 2) is 17, (-1, 2) is 22, and (2, -1) is 11.

10. C: The X value is -1 and the Y value is 0; this number is 15. (0, -1) is 20, (1, 0) is 12, (-1, -3) is 13, and (1, -3) is 18.

11. E: The X value is 2 and the Y value is -2; this number is 38. (-2, -2) is 34, (-2, 2) is 36, (2, 2) is 39, and (2, -3) is 35.

12. C: The X value is 1 and the Y value is -3; this number is 34. (-3, 1) is 31, (1, -1) is 38, (-1, 2) is 33, and (1, 3) is 36.

13. A: The X value is 3 and the Y value is 2; this number is is 38. (2, 3) is 34, (-3, 2) is 37, (3, -2) is 39, and (-3, -2) is 33.

14. A: The X value is 0 and the Y value is -1; this number is 39. (-1, 0) is 31, (0, -3) is 33, (-1, -3) is 32, and (0,2) is 34.

15. B: The X value is -2 and the Y value is -1; this number is 40. (2, 1) is 41, (-2, 1) is 35, (2, -1) is 37, and (-2, -3) is 31.

16. D: The X value is -3 and the Y value is 2; this number is 57. (2, -3) is 55, (3, -2) is 52, (-3, -2) is 53, and (2, 3) is 56.

17. D: The X value is -2 and the Y value is 0; this number is is 53. (0, -2) is 57, (2, 0) is 52, (0, 2) is 61, and (-2, -3) is 51.

18. A: The X value is 1 and the Y value is 1; this number is is 51. (-1, -1) is 57, (1, -1) is 52, (-1, 1) is 54, and (1, 3) is 55.

19. C: The X value is 2 and the Y value is -1; this number is 61. (-1, 2) is 56, (-2, -1) is 60, (2, 1) = 53, and (-2, 1) is 59.

20. B: The X value is -1 and the Y value is 3; this number is 53. (3, 1) is 55, (1, -1) is 52, (1, -3) is 54, and (-1, -1) is 57.

21. A: The X value is 0 and the Y value is 2; this number is 46. (2, 0) is 44, (0, -2) is 54, (-2, 0) is 48, and (0, -1) is 52.

22. C: The X value is 3 and the Y value is -2; this number is 45. (-2, 3) is 54, (-3, 2) is 50, (3, 2) is 49, and (-3, -2) is 42.

23. D: The X value is -1 and the Y value is 1; this number is 49. (1, -1) is 53, (-1, -1) is 45, (1, 1) is 51, and (-1, -3) is 42.

24. E: The X value is 2 and the Y value is 3; this number is 50. (3, 2) is 49, (-2, 3) is 54, (-2, -3) is 41, and (2, -3) is 45.

25. B: The X value is -2 and the Y value is 1; this number is 50. (1, -2) is 47, (2, -1) is 48, (-2, -1) is 46, and (2, 1) is 52.

26. E: The X value is 3 and the Y value is 0; this number is 16. (0,3) is 5, (-3, 0) is 10, (0, -3) is 8, and (3, -3) is 11.

27. B: The X value is 1 and the Y value is 2; this number is 6. (2, 1) is 17, (-1, 2) is 16, (1, -2) is 10, and (-1, -2) is 8.

28. C: The X value is -1 and the Y value is -1; this number is 10. (1, 1) is 16, (-1, 1) is 14, (1, -1) is 12, and (-1, -3) is 7.

29. C: The X value is -3 and the Y value is -2; this number is 6. (-2, -2) is 7, (3, -2) is 12, (-3, 2) is 14, and (3, 2) is 8.

30. A: The X value is 3 and the Y value is -1; this number is 14. (-1, 3) is 7, (3, 1) is 6, (-3, 1) is 12, and (-3, -1) is 8.

31. A: The X value is -3 and the Y value is -1; this number is 14. (-1, -3) is 13, (3, -1) is 20, (-3, 1) is 18, and (3, 1) = 12.

32. C: The X value is 0 and the Y value is 1; this number is 21. (1, 0) is 20, (0, -1) is 17, (-1, 0) is 18, and (0, -3) is 14.

33. E: The X value is 2 and the Y value is 1; this number is 11. (1, 2) is 12, (-2, 1) is 19, (2, -2) is 17, and (-2, -1) is 15.

34. B: The X value is 3 and the Y value is -3; this number is 17. (-3, 3) is 22, (3, 3) is 16, (-3, -3) is 11, and (3, -1) is 20.

35. D: The X value is -1 and the Y value is 2; this number is 22. (2, -1) is 19, (1, -2) is 16, (-1, -2) is 14, and (1, 2) is 12.

36. B: The X value is 2 and the Y value is 2; this number is 22. (-2, 2) is 30, (2, -2) is 26, (-2, -3) is 21, and (2, 1) is 20.

37. C: The X value is 1 and the Y value is -3; this number is 24. (-3, 1) is 27, (1, 3) is 23, (3, -1) is 29, and (-1, -3) is 22.

38. D: The X value is 1 and the Y value is -1; this number is 27. (1, 1) is 31, (-1, 1) is 29, (-1, -1) is 25, and (1, -3) is 24.

39. A: The X value is 2 and the Y value is -2; this number is 26. (-2, 2) is 30, (-2, -2) is 22, (2, 1) is 20, and (-2, -3) is 21.

40. B: The X value is 0 and the Y value is 3; this number is 22. (3, 0) is 31, (0, -3) is 23, (-3, 0) is 25, and (0, -1) is 26.

Block Counting

This section of the test measures your spatial reasoning and logic. You will be shown a three-dimensional (3-D) drawing of blocks. Some of these blocks may be touching, and, if so, you will be asked to determine the number of blocks that one particular block is touching. Keep in mind that some of the blocks may not be visible. There is no prior knowledge of block counting that is needed for this section of the test; just use logic and spatial reasoning.

In order for a block to "touch" another block, their faces must touch. If only two blocks' corners touch and not their faces, then they are not considered to be touching.

See the example problem below.

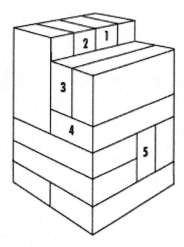

In this example, you know that Block 1 is touching 5 and other blocks. Block 1 is touching Block 2 and 3, the block to the right of Block 1, Block 4, and Block 5.

Block 2 is also touching 5 blocks: Block 1, the block to the left of Block 2, Block 3, Block 4, and one of the horizontal blocks beside Block 5.

What about Block 4? Block 4 is touching an astonishing 9 blocks: Block 3, the block to the right of Block 3, Blocks 1 and 2 and the two on either side of them, Block 5 and the two blocks on the left of it, and the one block on the right of Block 5.

Sometimes you will have to infer how big a block is when only part of the block is shown.

Practice Questions

For questions 1-30, determine how many blocks the given block is touching.

Use the figure below for questions 1-5.

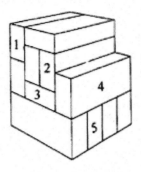

1. Block 1
    a. 1
    b. 2
    c. 3
    d. 4
    e. 5

2. Block 2
    a. 4
    b. 5
    c. 6
    d. 7
    e. 8

3. Block 3
    a. 5
    b. 6
    c. 7
    d. 8
    e. 9

4. Block 4
    a. 4
    b. 5
    c. 6
    d. 7
    e. 8

5. Block 5
   a. 2
   b. 3
   c. 4
   d. 5
   e. 6

Use the figure below for questions 6-10.

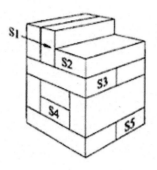

6. Block S1
   a. 1
   b. 2
   c. 3
   d. 4
   e. 5

7. Block S2
   a. 2
   b. 3
   c. 4
   d. 5
   e. 6

8. Block S3
   a. 5
   b. 6
   c. 7
   d. 8
   e. 9

9. Block S4
   a. 4
   b. 5
   c. 6
   d. 7
   e. 8

10. Block S5
   a. 3
   b. 4
   c. 5
   d. 6
   e. 7

Use the figure below for questions 11-17.

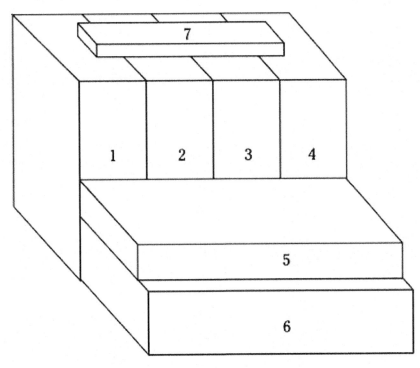

11. Block 1
   a. 1
   b. 2
   c. 3
   d. 4
   e. 5

12. Block 2
   a. 4
   b. 5
   c. 6
   d. 7
   e. 8

13. Block 3
   a. 5
   b. 6
   c. 7
   d. 2
   e. 1

14. Block 4
   a. 4
   b. 5
   c. 6
   d. 7
   e. 2

15. Block 5
    a. 2
    b. 3
    c. 4
    d. 5
    e. 6

    a. 3
    b. 4
    c. 5
    d. 6
    e. 7

16. Block 6
    a. 1
    b. 2
    c. 3
    d. 4
    e. 5

17. Block 7

Use the figure below for questions 18-22.

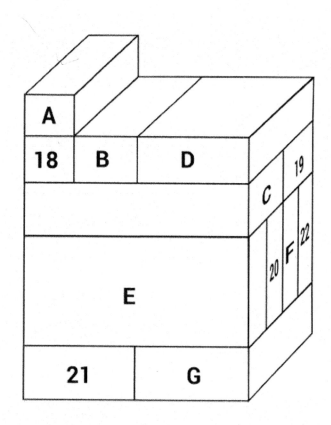

18. Block 18
    a. 1
    b. 2
    c. 3
    d. 4
    e. 5

19. Block 19
    a. 2
    b. 3
    c. 4
    d. 5
    e. 6

20. Block 20
   a. 1
   b. 2
   c. 3
   d. 4
   e. 5

21. Block 21
   a. 5
   b. 6
   c. 7
   d. 8
   e. 9

22. Block 22
   a. 4
   b. 5
   c. 6
   d. 7
   e. 8

Use the figure below for questions 23-26.

23. Block 1
   a. 1
   b. 2
   c. 3
   d. 4
   e. 5

24. Block 2
   a. 5
   b. 6
   c. 7
   d. 8
   e. 9

25. Block 3
   a. 4
   b. 5
   c. 6
   d. 7
   e. 8

26. Block 4
   a. 2
   b. 3
   c. 4
   d. 5
   e. 6

Use the figure below for questions 27-30.

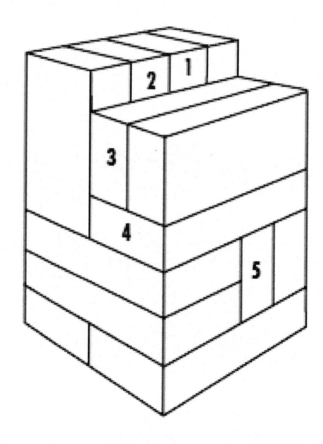

27. Block 1
   a. 1
   b. 2
   c. 3
   d. 4
   e. 5

28. Block 2
   a. 4
   b. 5
   c. 6
   d. 7
   e. 8

29. Block 3
   a. 2
   b. 3
   c. 4
   d. 5
   e. 6

30. Block 4
   a. 6
   b. 7
   c. 8
   d. 9
   e. 10

Answer Explanations

1. C: Block 1 touches 3 blocks: block below Block 1 and 2 blocks on the right side.

2. A: Block 2 touches 4 blocks: block above Block 2, block on the left of Block 2, Block 3, and Block 4.

3. D: Block 3 touches 8 blocks: 4 blocks on the bottom (including Block 5), Block 4, Block 2, block on the left of Block 2, and block below Block 1.

4. C: Block 4 touches 6 blocks: 4 blocks below (including Block 5), Block 2, and Block 3.

5. D: Block 5 touches 5 blocks: block on the left of Block 5, block on the right of Block 5, Block 4, Block 3, and block below Block 1.

6. D: Block S1 touches 4 blocks: block on the left of Block S1, Block S2, Block S3, and block on the right of Block S3.

7. B: Block S2 touches 3 blocks: Block S1, Block S3, and block on the right of Block S3.

8. C: Block S3 touches 7 blocks: block on the left of Block S1, Block S1, Block S2, block on the right of Block S3, block above Block S4, block on the left of Block S4, and block on the right of Block S4.

9. D: Block S4 touches 5 blocks: Block S5, block on the left of Block S5, block on the left of Block S4, block on right of Block S4, and block above Block S4.

10. B: Block S5 touches 4 blocks: block on the left of Block S5, block above Block S5, Block S4, and block on the left of Block S4.

11. D: Block 1 touches 4 blocks: Blocks 2, 5, 6, and 7.

12. B: Block 2 touches 5 blocks: Blocks 1, 3, 5, 6, and 7.

13. A: Block 3 touches 5 blocks: Blocks 2, 4, 5, 6, and 7.

14. A: Block 4 touches 4 blocks: Blocks 3, 5, 6, and 7.

15. D: Block 5 touches 5 blocks: Blocks 1, 2, 3, 4, and 6.

16. E: Block 6 touches 5 blocks: Blocks 1, 2, 3, 4, and 5.

17. B: Block 7 touches 4 blocks: Blocks 1, 2, 3, and 4.

18. D: Block 18 touches 4 blocks: Blocks A, B, C, and 19.

19. E: Block 19 touches 6 blocks: Blocks D, C, B, 18, 22, and F.

20. E: Block 20 touches 5 blocks: Blocks C, E,F, G, and 21.

21. A: Block 21 touches 5 blocks: Blocks E, G, 20, F, and 22.

22. A: Block 22 touches 4 blocks: Blocks 19, F, G, and 21.

23. C: Block 1 touches 3 blocks: block above Block 1, Block 3, and block to the left of Block 3.

24. C: Block 2 touches 7 blocks: block to the left of Block 5, Block 5, block to the left of Block 3, Block 3, 2 blocks to the back and left of Block 2, and Block 4.

25. D: Block 3 touches 7 blocks: Block 1, block above Block 1, block to the left of Block 3, Block 2, Block 4, and 2 blocks to the back and left of Block 2.

26. D: Block 4 touches 5 blocks: block to the left of Block 5, Block 5, block to the left of Block 3, Block 3, and Block 2.

27. E: Block 1 touches 5 blocks: Block 2, block to the right of Block 1, Block 3, Block 4, and Block 5.

28. B: Block 2 touches 5 blocks: block to the left of Block 2, Block 1, Block 3, Block 4, and the block below Block 4 and to the left of Block 5.

29. E: Block 3 touches 6 blocks: block to the left of Block 2, Block 2, Block 1, block to the right of Block 1, block to the right of Block 3, and Block 4.

30. D: Block 4 touches 9 blocks: block to the left of Block 2, Block 2, Block 1, block to the right of Block 1, Block 3, block to the right of Block 3, block below Block 4 and to the left of Block 5, Block 5, and block to the right of Block 5.

Instrument Comprehension

Purpose of Instrument-Comprehension Questions

The purpose of the instrument-comprehension questions is to ensure that vital instruments are understood. There needs to be a familiarity with the instruments and knowledge of their purposes, as well as how to read them.

Presentation of the Instrument-Comprehension Questions

Depending on the types of instruments covered in the test, the comprehension questions will vary in layout. For example, the practice questions in this section pertain to the artificial horizon and the compass. These two instruments are presented with the readings that you would need to be able to translate in order to determine the orientation of the aircraft, were they presented to you in the cockpit.

Reading the Compass and Artificial-Horizon Instruments

The compass on an aircraft is a navigational instrument used to determine the direction of flight, or the "aircraft heading." Compass reading is simple. As most people are aware, the needle reflects the direction being faced. When the aircraft is facing north, the needle will be pointing at the "N." If the aircraft is facing southwest, the needle will point to "SW."

The artificial horizon, also known as the attitude indicator, is an aircraft instrument that shows the aircraft orientation as compared with the Earth's horizon. This instrument indicates the pitch and bank of the aircraft, which is the tilt of the nose and the wings. The artificial horizon becomes relatively easy to read and interpret once you visualize it from the pilot seat.

The artificial horizon utilizes a small airplane or wings and a horizon bar. The aircraft in the instrument is representative of the host aircraft that is being flown. The horizon bar represents the actual horizon of the Earth. Many artificial-horizon instruments are blue in the upper half representing the sky and dark on the lower half, which represents the ground. If the aircraft or wings in the instrument are above the horizon bar, the aircraft is nose up or climbing. If the aircraft is shown below the horizon bar in the instrument, then the aircraft is nose down, or descending in altitude. When the symbolic aircraft is even with the horizon bar, the plane is in level flight.

The artificial-horizon instrument typically will have degree marks that indicate the amount of aircraft banking that occurs during turning maneuvers. The horizon bar will tilt opposite of the direction of the wings, which will show the orientation of the aircraft to the horizon during banking.

The questions in this section will provide compass and artificial-horizon indications instruments (see example below), and you will be required to determine the orientation of the aircraft using these two. Besides looking at the compass for direction, pay close attention to the artificial horizon to determine if the indication is that of a climbing or descending aircraft, or possibly an aircraft in level flight. Also it is important to verify the direction of banking. Once you have figured out the heading, the pitch, and the banking, you should be able to choose the correct answer from the simulated aircraft images provided.

For the purpose of these questions, the simulated aircraft will appear to be flying away from your view for north, facing you for south, facing with the nose to left of the page for west and to the right for east.

Example practice question: Looking at the instruments on the left, which choice depicts the orientation of the aircraft?

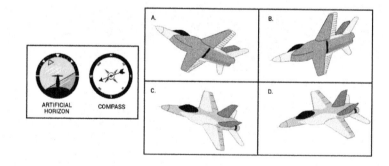

The correct answer to the example question is "A". The compass is showing a west-southwest heading. The artificial horizon shows the wings are above the horizon bar, indicating the aircraft is in a climb. Lastly, the artificial horizon shows the right wing is dipped, as the horizon bar is tilted opposite. This indicates the aircraft is banked to the right. Put it all together and you have an aircraft heading west-southwest (facing away and to the left), while it is in a climb and a right bank. The only choice that corresponds to this orientation is answer A.

Studying for the compass and artificial horizon portion of the test

You may want to practice with a standard compass if you are not familiar with compass reading. Many smartphones have compass capabilities, or you can find one at a sporting-goods store. You probably will not be able to find an artificial horizon to practice with, so it is recommended that you prepare for this portion of the test using the following practice questions.

Practice Questions

1. Looking at the instruments on the left, which choice depicts the orientation of the aircraft?

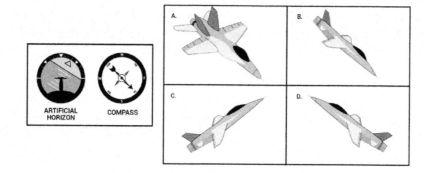

2. Looking at the instruments on the left, which choice depicts the orientation of the aircraft?

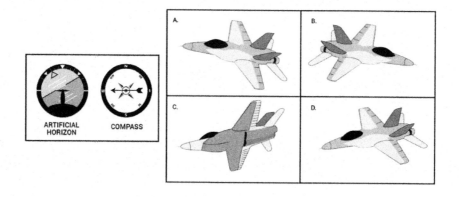

3. Looking at the instruments on the left, which choice depicts the orientation of the aircraft?

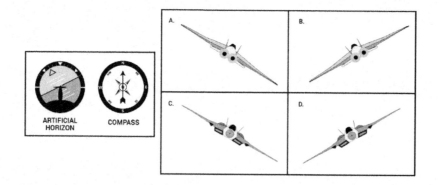

4. Looking at the instruments on the left, which choice depicts the orientation of the aircraft?

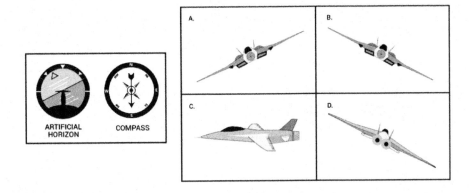

5. Looking at the instruments on the left, which choice depicts the orientation of the aircraft?

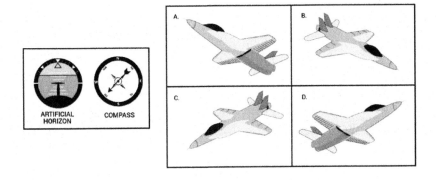

6. Looking at the instruments on the left, which choice depicts the orientation of the aircraft?

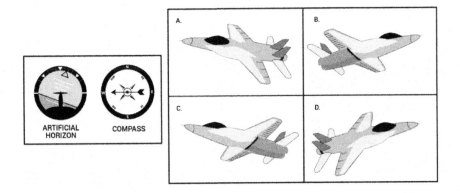

7. Looking at the instruments on the left, which choice depicts the orientation of the aircraft?

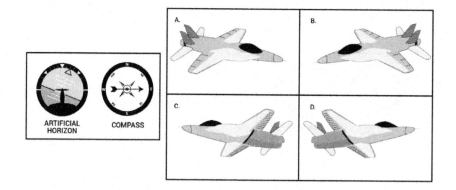

8. Looking at the instruments on the left, which choice depicts the orientation of the aircraft?

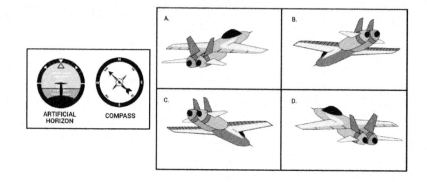

9. Looking at the instruments on the left, which choice depicts the orientation of the aircraft?

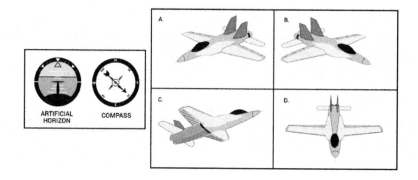

10. Looking at the instruments on the left, which choice depicts the orientation of the aircraft?

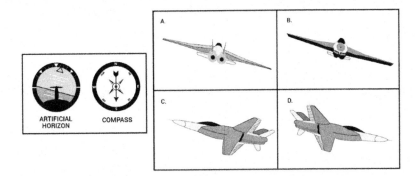

Answers Explanations

1. B: The aircraft is heading southeast, descending, and banking left.

2. C: The aircraft is heading west, descending, and banking right.

3. A: The aircraft is heading north, in level flight, and banking right.

4. A: The aircraft is heading south, in level flight, and banking to the right.

5. C: The aircraft is heading southwest, descending, and without banking.

6. A: The aircraft is heading west, ascending, and banking left.

7. D: The aircraft is heading east, ascending, and banking left.

8. D: The aircraft is heading northwest, ascending, and without banking.

9. B: The aircraft is heading southeast, descending, and without banking.

10. B: The aircraft is heading south, ascending, and banking left.

Aviation Information

The aviation information contained in this section can help provide some basic knowledge in the following areas:

- Fixed-wing aircraft
- Flight envelope
- Flight concepts and terminology
- Flight maneuvers
- Helicopters
- Airport information

Fixed-wing aircraft

A fixed-wing aircraft is one in which movement of the wings in relation to the aircraft is not used to generate lift, even though technically they flex in flight, as do all wings. In contrast, helicopters generate lift through rotating airfoils.

Fixed-wing aircraft have the following items in common: wings, flight controls, tail assembly, landing gear, fuselage, and an engine or powerplant. Here's an illustration of many of the parts of planes:

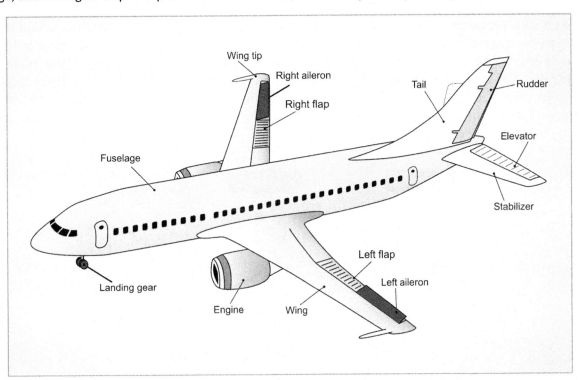

Wings

An airfoil is a surface such as a wing, elevator, or aileron that is designed to help create lift and control of an aircraft by using and manipulating air flow. The standard wing, or airfoil, is mounted to the sides of the fuselage. The outline or cross section of the airfoil is referred to as the airfoil profile. The standard wing has an upper surface that is curved while the lower surface is relatively flat. The air moves over the curved surface of the wing at a higher speed than it moves under the flat surface. The difference in airflow on the surfaces of the wing creates lift due to the aircraft's forward airspeed, which enables flight.

Many modern aircraft structures use full cantilever wings, meaning no external bracing is required. The strength in this design is from the internal structural members and the fuselage. Semi-cantilever wings use some form of external bracing, whether it be wires or struts.

Aircraft wing designs vary based on the characteristics and type of performance needed for the aircraft. Changing the wing design changes the amount of lift that can be created and the amount of stability and control the aircraft will have at different speeds. Some aircraft have wings that are designed to tilt, sweep, or fold. So long as they do not generate lift, they are still considered fixed-wing aircraft. Wing geometry is related to the shape of the aircraft wings when viewed from the front of the aircraft, or from above.

Flight Controls
Flight controls, like the name implies, are used to direct the forces on an aircraft in flight for the purpose of directional and attitude control. Flight controls vary from simple mechanical (manually operated) systems, to hydro-mechanical systems, to fly-by-wire systems. Fly-by-wire systems send signal via wire to control the plane.

When discussing flight controls, it's important to understand the terms *leading edge* and *trailing edge*. *Leading edge* refers to the front part of the wing that separates air, forcing it to go above or below the wing. *Trailing edge* is the back part of the wing and where the air comes back together.

The flight controls typically are divided into primary and secondary systems.

The primary flight controls are responsible for the movement of the aircraft along its three axes of flight. Primary flight controls on an aircraft are the *elevators, ailerons,* and *rudder.* Elevators are mounted on the trailing edges of horizontal stabilizers and are used for controlling aircraft pitch about the lateral axis. The ailerons are mounted on the trailing edges of the wings and are used for controlling aircraft roll about the longitudinal axis. The rudder is mounted on the trailing edge of the vertical fin and is used for controlling rotation (yaw) around the vertical axis. Here's an illustration of pitch, roll, and yaw along the three axes.

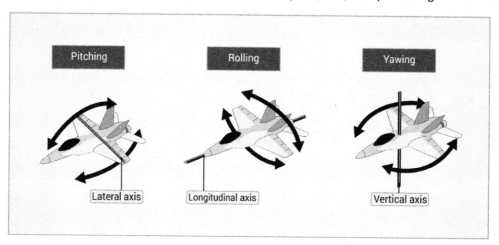

Secondary, or auxiliary, flight controls include (but are not limited to): flaps, slats, spoilers, speed brakes, and the trim system. Flaps are the hinged portion of the wing trailing edge between the ailerons and the fuselage, and sometimes may be located on the leading edge of a wing as well. If used during takeoff, flaps reduce the amount of runway and time needed to takeoff. During landings, flaps increase the drag on the wings slowing the plane down and allowing it to go slower right before it lands, which then reduces the amount of runway needed. Essentially, flaps allow the aircraft to produce more lift at slower airspeeds. Flaps are also utilized on some planes to increase maneuverability. The amount of flap extension and the angle can be adjusted by the flap levers located in the cockpit.

Spoilers are located on the upper, or trailing edge, of the wing and are used to decrease lift. They allow the nose of the aircraft to be pitched down without increasing the airspeed, allowing for a safe landing speed. Slats are located on the middle to outboard portion of the leading edge of the wing. They are used to create additional lift and slower flight by extending the shape of the wing. Flaps and slats are hidden inside the wing and are extended during takeoff and landing.

The trim system is an inexpensive autopilot that eliminates the need for the pilot to constantly maintain pressure on the controls. Most aircraft trim systems contain trim, balance, anti-balance, and servo tabs. These tabs are found on the trailing edge of primary flight control surfaces and are used to counteract hydro-mechanical and aerodynamic forces acting on the aircraft.

Tail Assembly
The tail assembly of an aircraft is commonly referred to as the empennage. The empennage structure typically includes a tail cone, fixed stabilizers (horizontal and vertical), and moveable surfaces to assist in directional control. The moveable surfaces are the rudder, which is attached to the vertical stabilizer, and the elevators attached to the horizontal stabilizers.

Landing Gear
Aircraft require landing gear not only for takeoffs and landings but also to support the aircraft while it is on the ground. The landing gear must be designed to support the entire weight of the aircraft and handle the loads placed on it during landing, as well as be as light as possible. Small aircraft that fly at low-speeds usually have fixed landing gear, which means it is stationary and does not have the ability to retract in flight. Aircraft that fly at higher speeds require retractable landing gear so that the gear is not in the airstream. Retractable landing gear makes the aircraft more aerodynamic by reducing drag, but usually at the cost of additional weight when compared to the fixed landing gear. Also, the landing gear should only be operated (extended or retracted) when the airspeed indicator is at or below the aircraft's maximum landing-gear operating speed, or V_{LO}. Airspeeds above V_{LO} can damage the landing gear operating mechanism. When the gear is down and locked, the aircraft should not be operated above the aircraft's maximum landing-gear extended speed, or V_{LE}. Since landing gear is more stable when all the way down than when being moved, V_{LE} will be higher for an aircraft than V_{LO}. A switch or lever that resembles the shape of a wheel is used to raise and lower the landing gear.

Landing gear is made from a variety of materials, such as magnesium, steel, and aluminum. Most landing gear has some type of shock absorbers and braking system. Not all landing gear uses wheels. Depending on what the aircraft is used for, it may have skis, skids, pontoons, or floats instead of tires for landing on snow, ice, or water.

Landing gear is typically found in two configurations: tricycle gear and conventional gear (also known as tail wheel gear).

Tricycle gear is the most common configuration. Tricycle gear has a single wheel in the front (usually under the nose) and two wheels side-by-side at the center of gravity of the aircraft. Large, heavy aircraft may contain extra wheels in this configuration. Small aircraft equipped with nose landing gear can typically be steered with rudder pedals.

Conventional tail wheel aircraft or "tail draggers" were more common in the early days of aviation. The two main wheels supported the heaviest portion of the aircraft, with the third smaller wheel was near the tail. Having the smaller wheel in the tail allowed the aircraft to rest at an incline on the ground, which provided more clearance for the nose propeller. In some conventional gear, the tail wheel could be steered mechanically with the rudder pedals.

Fuselage
The fuselage is the main structure, or airframe, of an aircraft. The fuselage is where the cockpit, or cabin, of the aircraft is, and where passengers or cargo may be located. It provides attachment points for the main

components of the aircraft such as the wings, engines, and empennage. If an aircraft is a single-engine, the fuselage houses the powerplant as well. If the powerplant is a reciprocating engine, it is mounted in the front of the aircraft, while a turbine engine would be mounted in the rear of the aircraft. *Cowling* is the term for the covering of an airplane's engine which is streamlined to maximize aerodynamics.

Aircraft contain a battery that is charged by an alternator or generator. Wiring takes the electric current to where it's needed throughout the plane. Some type of warning system will be in place to warn of inadequate current output. This could be a warning light or an ammeter. If the number showing on an ammeter is positive, it means the battery is charging. If the number is negative, it means that the alternator or generator cannot keep up with the amount of current being used. Some aircraft have a loadmeter, which shows the amount of current being drawn from the battery.

Fuselage structures are usually classified as truss, monocoque, and semi-monocoque. The truss fuselage is typically made of steel tubing welded together, which enables the structure to handle tension and compression loads. In lighter aircraft, an aluminum alloy may be used along with cross-bracing. A single shell fuselage is referred to as monocoque, which uses a stronger skin to handle the tension and compression loads. There is also a semi-monocoque fuselage, which is basically a combination of the truss and monocoque fuselage, and is the most commonly used.

Powerplant

The powerplant of an aircraft is its engine, which is a component of the propulsion system that generates mechanical power and thrust. Most modern aircraft engines are typically either turbine or piston engines.

Flight Envelope

The flight envelope (also known as the performance envelope or service envelope) refers to the capabilities of an aircraft based on its design in terms of altitude, airspeed, loading factors, and maneuverability. When an aircraft is pushed to the point it exceeds design limitations for that specific aircraft, it is considered to be operating outside the envelope, which is considered dangerous.

All aircraft have approved flight manuals that contain the flight limitations or parameters. To ensure an aircraft is being operated properly, a pilot needs to be familiar with the aircraft's flight envelope prior to flight. The flight parameters are based on the engine and wing design and include the following: maximum and minimum speed, stall speed, climb rate, glide ratio, maximum altitude, and the maximum amount of gravity forces (g-forces) the aircraft can withstand.

- The *maximum speed* of an aircraft is based on air resistance getting lower at higher altitudes, to a point where increased altitude no longer increases maximum speed due to lack of oxygen to "feed" the engine.

- The stalling speed is the minimum speed at which an aircraft can maintain level flight. As the aircraft gains altitude, the stall speed increases (since the aircraft's weight can be better supported through speed).

- The *climb rate* is the vertical speed of an aircraft, which is the increase in altitude in respect to time.

- The *climb gradient* is the ratio of the increase in altitude to the horizontal air distance.

- The *glide ratio* is the ratio of horizontal distance traveled per rate of fall.

- The *maximum altitude* of an aircraft is also referred to as the service ceiling. The ceiling is usually determined by the aircraft performance and the wings, and is where an altitude at a given speed can no longer be increased at level flight.

- The *maximum g-forces* each aircraft can withstand varies, but is based on its design and structural strength.

Commercial aircraft are considered to have a small flight envelope, since the range of speed and maneuverability is rather limited, and they are designed to operate efficiently under moderate conditions. The Federal Aviation Administration (FAA) is the controlling body in the United States pertaining to authorized flight envelopes and restrictions for commercial and civilian aircraft. The FAA may reduce a flight envelope for added safety as needed.

Military aircraft, especially fighter jets, have extremely large flight envelopes. By design, these aircraft are very maneuverable and can operate at high speeds as their purpose requires. The term "pushing the envelope" originally referred to military pilots taking an aircraft to the extreme limits of their capabilities, mostly during combat, but also during aircraft flight testing. The term "outside the envelope" is when the aircraft is pushed outside the design specifications and is considered very dangerous. Operating outside the limits of the aircraft can severely degrade the life of components, or even lead to mechanical failure.

Some of the modern fly-by-wire aircraft have built in flight envelope protection. This protection is built into the control system and helps prevent a pilot from forcing an aircraft into a situation that exceeds its structural and aerodynamic operational limits. This system is beneficial in emergency situations because it prevents the pilots from endangering the aircraft while making split-second decisions.

Flight Concepts and Terminology

Aerodynamics is the study of objects in motion through the air, such as when the air interacts with an aircraft wing, and the forces that produce or change such motion. It is important to note that the air affects the aerodynamics of an aircraft in flight. Therefore, it is important that the aircraft's operating environment, the atmosphere, is understood.

Atmospheric pressure differs depending on altitude. The higher the altitude above sea level, the less pressure exists. Air density varies with pressure. The higher the altitude, the less dense the air. Humidity, the amount of water vapor in the air, varies with the temperature.

There are four main forces that act on all aircraft: *gravity, lift, thrust,* and *drag.* The four main forces are always present during aircraft flight. For flight to occur, thrust and lift always need to be greater than the gravity and drag forces.

Gravity

Gravity is the downward force that pulls everything toward the surface of the Earth at a rate of 9.8 m/s^2. The weight of an object's mass is the result of gravity acting upon the object. The pull is also called the weight force. Aircraft need to provide enough lift force to overcome gravity to fly.

Lift

The *lift* force is created by the motion of the aircraft through the air. The air that travels over the curved surface of a wing has farther to go than the air moving below the wing. The air above must travel faster than the air below to reach the back of the wing at the same time. The air traveling faster over the top of a wing creates lower pressure. The lower pressure above the wing causes it to lift. *Bernoulli's principle* illustrates that an increase in velocity is always accompanied by a decrease in pressure and creates lift on an airfoil.

Thrust

The engine, or powerplant, of the aircraft creates thrust, which is necessary to create forward motion. *Thrust* is the force that propels the aircraft forward to provide airflow beneath the wings for lift. The purpose of thrust is not to lift an aircraft, but to overcome the force of drag. The direction of thrust can be varied by the design of the aircraft propulsion system.

Drag

Drag is the force generated when an aircraft is moving through the air. Drag is air resistance that opposes thrust, basically aerodynamic friction or wind resistance. The amount of drag is dependent on several factors, including the shape of the aircraft, the speed it is traveling, and the density of the air it is passing through. There are two categories of drag: *induced drag* and *parasitic drag*. Induced drag is created through the generation of lift and is caused by wingtip vortices (rotating air coming off wings). Parasitic drag is created by the shape of the aircraft.

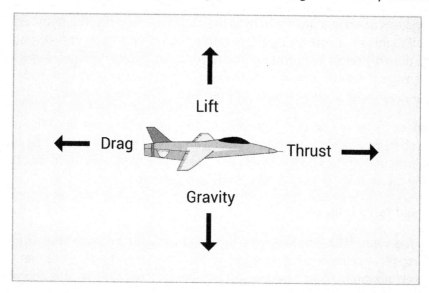

The angular difference measured between an aircraft's axis and the line of the horizon is the flight attitude. Aircraft attitude is based on relative positions of the nose and wings on the natural horizon. There are four types of attitude flying: pitch control, bank control, power control, and trim control. The angle formed by the longitudinal axis of the aircraft is pitch attitude. The angle formed by the lateral axis is bank attitude. Yaw is the rotation of the aircraft around its vertical axis, which is not relative to the horizon, but to the flightpath. Power control is used when there is a need for a change in thrust in the aircraft. Trim is for relieving all possible control pressures held after the desired attitude has been reached. The moveable surfaces on the wings and tail introduced earlier allow for control of an aircraft's attitude and orientation. These airfoils work on the same principle as the lift on the wing.

Here are some examples of pitch control and bank control:

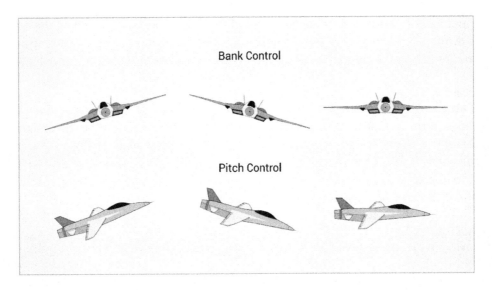

Bank Control

Pitch Control

Flight Controls and Forces

The vertical stabilizer, or the tail fin, keeps the aircraft aligned in the desired direction. Air presses on both sides of the tail with equal force when operating in a straight line. When the aircraft yaws left or right, the air pressure increases on one side of the tail and decreases on the other side. The imbalance of the pressure acting upon the tail will push it back in line.

The horizontal stabilizer provides for leveling of an aircraft in flight. If the aircraft tilts up or down, the air pressure increases on one side of the stabilizer and decreases on the other. This imbalance on the stabilizer will push the aircraft back into level flight. The horizontal stabilizer holds the tail down as well, since most aircraft designs induce a tendency for the nose to tilt down due to the center of gravity being forward of the center of lift.

Ailerons are located on the outer, trailing edges of the wings, and control the roll of an aircraft. The ailerons operate opposite each other, up and down, to decrease lift on one wing and increase lift on the other. The change in lift will cause the aircraft to roll either to the left or right; therefore, the pilot will use the ailerons to tilt the aircraft in the direction of a turn.

The elevators are moveable control surfaces attached to the trailing edge of the horizontal stabilizer. The elevators tilt up and down to increase or decrease lift on the tail. The increase or decrease in lift will cause the nose of the aircraft to tilt up or down.

The rudder is a moveable control surface located on the aft end of the aircraft vertical tail fin. The rudder moves from side to side, pushing the tail left or right. The rudder is used in conjunction with the ailerons to turn an aircraft.

Trim Control

In-flight variable trim control along the three axes is used to level an aircraft in pitch and roll while eliminating yaw. The trim system serves to counter the aerodynamic forces that affect the balance of the aircraft in flight. The control pressures on an aircraft change as conditions change during a flight. Trim control systems can compensate for the change in weight and center of gravity that occurs in flight as the aircraft burns fuel, as well as compensating for change in wind and atmospheric pressure. Trim can relieve all possible control pressures held after the desired attitude has been reached. Larger and more sophisticated aircraft tend to have a more sophisticated trim system in the pitch, roll, and yaw axes. Smaller aircraft tend to have only pitch control.

The primary flight controls are positioned in-line with the aircraft surfaces during straight-and-level flight. When the flight is not balanced, one or more flight control surfaces will need to be adjusted by continuous control input. This input can be performed through the use of trim tabs; therefore, avoiding the need for constant adjustments by the pilot. The trim systems also prevent the pilot from having to exert strong control force for an extended amount of time—essentially easing the physical workload required to control the aircraft.

Angle of Attack

The angle of attack (AOA) is the angle between the relative wind and the chord line (line between the leading and trailing edge of the airfoil). The AOA can be used to affect the amount of lift on an aircraft. The greater the AOA, the greater the lift generated until the AOA reaches the critical angle of attack. The critical angle of attack induces a stall because the induced drag exceeds the lift. During a stall, the wing is no longer able to create sufficient lift to oppose gravity. Stall angle is usually around 20°. Thus once it's been reached, any subsequent increase in the AOA hurts aerodynamics.

Additional Related Terms

Center of gravity: In flight, the aircraft rotates around its center of gravity.

Ground effect: The reduced drag and increased lift that is experienced by an aircraft flying in close proximity to the ground is called the ground effect. For fixed-wing aircraft it is considered in ground effect when the wing is in close proximity of the ground. A helicopter is considered to be in ground effect when it is within one rotor diameter of the ground. For example, if the rotor diameter of the helicopter is 50 feet, then 50 feet and below is considered to be in ground effect.

Flight Maneuvers

There are four fundamental maneuvers in flight: straight-and-level, turns, climbs, and descents. Every controlled flight usually includes a combination of these four fundamentals.

The duration and the amount of pressure used on the flight controls determine the displacement of the corresponding flight control, which controls the maneuver being made. Since the airspeed differs during maneuvers, the distance the flight controls move is not as important as the appropriate pressure the pilot applies to the control for each maneuver.

Straight-and-Level Flight

Maintaining a heading and altitude, with only minor adjustments to flight controls, is referred to as straight-and-level flight. Straight-and-level flight may require adjustment depending on the atmospheric conditions — just as keeping an automobile going in a straight line can require adjustments. This laterally level flight can be achieved by checking the relationship of the aircraft wingtips with the natural horizon. The distance of both wingtips above or below the horizon should be the same. Any adjustments should be made with the ailerons. To a lesser extent, the wingtips can also be used to determine pitch attitude. During straight-and-level flight, small deviations from lateral flight can be addressed quickly with small corrections. Almost no control pressure is required to maintain straight-and-level if the aircraft is properly trimmed and is in smooth air. Airspeed will usually remain consistent when a constant power setting is used.

Turns

A turn in an aircraft is performed by banking the wings in the direction of the turn. The appropriate amount of control pressures need to be applied by the pilot to achieve and hold the desired banking for the turn. All primary controls are required and should be coordinated during a turn.

Turns are divided into three classes: shallow, medium, and steep. Shallow turns are typically less than 20°, which is so shallow that the aircraft's lateral stability acts to level the wings, unless an aileron is used to maintain banking. Medium turns range from approximately 20° to 45°, and the aircraft holds a constant bank. Steep turns are more than 45°, and the aircraft will have a tendency to overbank without the addition of aileron control.

During constant altitude and airspeed turns, the elevator should be up to increase the angle-of-attack (AOA) of the wing when rolling into a turn. Use of the elevator during a turn is needed because the vertical lift has been changed to a horizontal lift. To stop the turn, the aileron and rudder are used in the opposite direction to return the wings to level flight.

Climbs

An aircraft's climb is restricted by the amount of thrust available, since the thrust needs to be able to overcome the increased drag that occurs during climbing maneuvers. In a climb, the weight is no longer perpendicular to the flightpath; it is directed rearward.

Climbs require the simultaneous increase in throttle and back-pressure on the elevator to lift the nose of the aircraft. Nose-up elevator trim may be used after the climb has been established to make minor adjustments in pitch.

Descents

Descent is when an aircraft changes flight path to a downward inclined plane, normally losing altitude with partial power. The settings recommended by the aircraft manufacturer should be used when setting pitch and power for a descent. The power, pitch, and airspeed should be kept constant.

Helicopters

Helicopters, a type of rotary-wing or rotorcraft are extremely versatile aircraft that may be used for a wide array of situations where a typical aircraft could not perform. A helicopter differs from other types of aircraft that derive lift from their wings, as it gets its lift and thrust from the rotors. The rotors are basically rotating airfoils; hence the name rotorcraft. The "rotating wing," or main rotor, may have two or more blades whose profiles resemble that of aircraft wings.

Although rotorcraft come in many shapes and sizes, they mostly have the same major components in common. There is a cabin, an airframe, landing gear, a powerplant, a transmission, and an anti-torque system. The cabin of the rotorcraft houses the crew and cargo. The airframe is the fuselage where components are mounted and attached. The landing gear may be made up of wheels, skis, skids, or floats.

Due to its operating characteristics, a helicopter is able to:

- Take off and land vertically (in almost any small, clear area)
- Fly forward, backward, and laterally
- Operate at lower speeds
- Hover for extended periods of time

Common uses for the helicopter include military operations, search and rescue, law enforcement, firefighting, medical transport, news reporting, and tourism.

Helicopters are subjected to the same forces as other aircraft: lift, weight, thrust, and drag. In addition, helicopters also have some unique forces they are subjected to: torque, centrifugal and centripetal force, gyroscopic precession, dissymmetry of lift, effective translational lift, transverse flow effect, and Coriolis effect.

Examples of a variety of helicopters:

Torque

Torque from the engine turning the main rotor forces the body of the helicopter in the opposite direction. Most helicopters use a tail rotor, which counters this torque force by pushing or pulling against the tail.

Centrifugal and Centripetal Force

Centrifugal force is the force that causes rotating bodies to move away from the center of rotation. Centripetal force is the force that counteracts centrifugal force, since it keeps an object a certain distance from the center of rotation.

Gyroscopic Precession

Gyroscopic precession is when the applied force to a rotating object is shown 90º later than where the force was applied.

Dissymmetry of Lift

Dissymmetry of lift is the difference in lift between the advancing and retreating blades of the rotor system. The difference in lift is due to directional flight. The rotor system compensates for dissymmetry of lift with blade flapping, which allows the blades to twist and lift in order to balance the advancing and retreating blades. The pilot also compensates by cyclic feathering. Together, blade flapping and cyclic feathering eliminate dissymmetry of lift.

Effective Translational Lift

Effective translational lift (ETL) is the improved efficiency that results from directional flight. Efficiency is gained when the helicopter moves forward, as opposed to hovering. The incoming airflow essentially pushes the turbulent air behind the helicopter, which provides a more horizontal airflow for the airfoil to move through. This typically occurs between 16 and 24 knots.

Transverse Flow Effect

Transverse flow effect is the difference in airflow between the forward and aft portions of the rotor disk. During forward flight, there is more downwash in the rear portion of the rotor disk. The downward flow on the rear portion of the disk results in a reduced AOA and produces less lift. The front half of the rotor produces more lift due to an increased AOA. Transverse flow occurs between 10 and 20 knots and can be easily recognized by the increased vibrations during take-off and landing.

Coriolis Effect

The Coriolis Effect is when an object moving in a rotating system experiences an inertial force (Coriolis) acting perpendicular to the direction of motion and the axis of rotation. In a clockwise rotation, the force acts to the left of the motion of an object. If the rotation is counterclockwise, the force acts to the right of the motion of an object.

A typical helicopter is controlled through use of the cyclic control stick, the collective controls lever, and the anti-torque pedals.

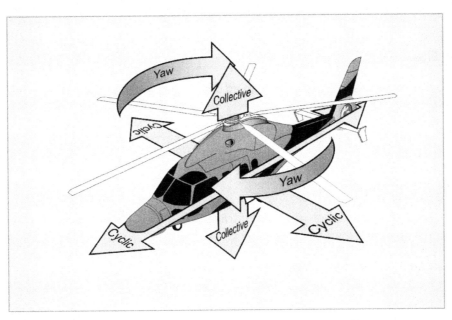

Cyclic Control

The cyclic is the control stick that is used to control the movement of the helicopter forward, backward, or sideways. Simply stated, the cyclic changes the pitch of the rotor blades cyclically in any of 360°. The cyclic stick also contains several buttons that control the trim, intercom, and radio. These will differ slightly depending on each model helicopter.

Collective Controls

The collective control is used to increase the pitch of the main rotor simultaneously at all points of the rotor blade rotation. The collective increases or decreases total rotor thrust; the cyclic changes the direction of rotor thrust. In forward flight, the collective pitch changes the amount of thrust, which in turn can change the speed or altitude based on the use of the cyclic. During hovering, the collective control is used to adjust the altitude of hover.

Anti-Torque Pedals

The anti-torque pedals are used to control yaw on a helicopter. These pedals are located in the same place, and serve a similar purpose, as rudder pedals on an airplane. Application of pressure on a pedal changes the pitch of the tail rotor blade, which will increase or reduce the tail rotor thrust and cause the nose of the helicopter to yaw in the desired direction.

Airport Information

Airports vary in size and complexity, from small dirt or grass strips to a large major airport with miles of paved runways and taxiways. Pilots are required to know the procedures and rules of the specific airports being used, and understand pavement markings, lights, and signs that provide takeoff, landing, and taxiway information.

Procedures have been developed for airport traffic patterns and traffic control. These procedures include specific routes or specific runways for takeoffs and landings. Each airport traffic pattern depends on a number of factors, including obstructions and wind conditions.

<u>Terms</u>

Clearway: A specified area after the runway that is clear of obstacles, at the same or nearly the same altitude as the runway, and specifically for planes to fly over in their initial ascent.

Decision height (DH): The lowest height (in feet) in which if a pilot cannot see specified visual references, they must stop landing

Holding/Flying a Hold: Refers to a plane flying in an oval flight path near the airport while waiting for clearance to land

Runway visual range (RVR): The distance away from the airport in which a pilot should be able to see runway markings and/or lights.

Threshold: The start or end of a runway

Taxiway: The paved area that planes travel on to travel between the terminal and runway. The path a plane should follow on a taxiway is marked by a yellow line

Taxiway intersections: Where two taxiway routes intersect.

<u>Signs</u>

Here are some common taxiway signs:

Name	Sign Color	Letter Color	Function
no entry	red	white	indicates an area planes should not go into
runway location	black	yellow	displays current runway name
taxiway location	black	yellow	displays current taxiway name
direction/runway exit	yellow	black	displays name of upcoming taxiway that airplane is about to intersect with
runway	red	white	displays name of runway that airplane is about to intersect with

<u>Lighting</u>

These lights are visible to about 3 miles in the daytime and up to 20 miles at night.

- *Approach Lighting Systems (ALS)*: A series of light bars leading up to a runway that assist the pilot in lining up with the runway.

- *Runway centerline lights*: There are used to facilitate landing at night or under adverse visibility conditions. These lights are embedded into the runway. They begin as white, then alternate between red and white, and then are completely red at the end of the runway.

- *Obstructions/aircraft warning lights*: *Red* or *white* lights used to mark obstructions (like building and cell towers) both in airports and outside of them.

- *Runway edge lights*: These are *white* and highlight the boundaries of the runway. These are referred to a high, medium, or low intensity depending on the maximum intensity they can produce.

- *Runway end identifier lights (REIL)*: Many airport runways have these two flashing *red* lights. They provide a warning that the runway is ending.

- *Taxiway centerline lights*: *Green* lights indicating the middle of a taxiway.

- *Taxiway edge lights*: *Blue* lights denoting the edge of a taxiway.

- *Threshold lights*: *Green* lights that indicate the start of the runway

Visual Approach Slope Indicators (VASI)

The visual approach slope indicator (VASI) is a light system of two sets of lights designed to provide visual guidance during approach of a runway. The light indicators are visible 3-5 miles away during daylight hours and up to 20 miles away in darkness. The indicators are designed to be used once the aircraft is already visually aligned with the runway. Both sets of lights can appear as white or red. When the front lights appear white and the back lights appear red, it indicates that the plane is at the proper angle. If both lights appear white, it means the pilot is too high, and if both appear red, it means the pilot is too low.

Precision Instrument Runways

Precision instrument runways have operational visual and electronic aids that provide directional guidance. These aides may be the ILS, Precision Approach Radar (PAR), or Microwave Landing System (MLS). Instrument runways have visual aids with a decision height greater than 200 feet and a runway visual range of 2,600 feet. These runways have *runway end lights*, which consists of eight lights (four on each side of the runway) that can appear as green or red—green to approaching planes and red to planes on the runway.

Non-Precision Instrument Runways

Non-precision instrument runways provide horizontal guidance only when there is an approved procedure for a straight-in non-precision instrument approach. The non-precision runways do not have full Instrument Landing System (ILS) capabilities, but they have approved procedures for localizer, Global Positioning System (GPS), Automatic Direction Finder (ADF), and Very High Frequency Omni-Directional Range (VOR) instrument approaches.

Visual Flight Rules Runways (VFR)

Visual flight rules (VFR) runways, also known as visual runways, operate completely under visual approach procedures. The pilot must be able to see the runway to land safely. There are no instrument approach procedures for this type of runway. They are typically found at small airports. Visual runways have centerline, designators, and threshold markings, as well as hold position markings for taxiway intersections.

Localizer Type Directional Aid (LDA)

Directional runways use a Localizer Type Directional Aid (LDA). The LDA provides a localizer-based instrument approach to an airport where, usually due to terrain, the localizer antenna is not in alignment with the runway. The LDA is more of a directional tool to enable the pilot to get close enough to where the runway can be seen.

Practice Questions

1. Which of the following will create lift?
   a. Airflow against the tail section of the aircraft
   b. Faster flow of air over the wing than beneath it
   c. Raised ailerons
   d. Helium in the wings
   e. Thrust from the engine

2. Which of the following axes is controlled by ailerons?
   a. Lateral
   b. Longitudinal
   c. Vertical
   d. Equatorial
   e. Felling axes

3. Which of the following axes is controlled by elevators?
   a. Lateral
   b. Longitudinal
   c. Vertical
   d. Equatorial
   e. All of the above

4. Which of the following axes is controlled by a rudder?
   a. Lateral
   b. Longitudinal
   c. Vertical
   d. Equatorial
   e. None of the above

5. Which of the following is not a secondary or auxiliary flight control?
   a. Flap
   b. Spoiler
   c. Aileron
   d. Slat
   e. All of the above

6. What component is not part of an empennage?
   a. Stabilizer
   b. Rudder
   c. Elevator
   d. Truss
   e. Slats

7. Which of the following is not a type of landing gear?
   a. Ski
   b. Skate
   c. Skid
   d. Float
   e. Pontoon

8. Which is not a type of fuselage?
   a. Monocoque
   b. Semicoque
   c. Semi-Monocoque
   d. Truss
   e. None of the above

9. Who should be the most concerned about an aircraft's flight envelope?
   a. The pilot
   b. Air traffic controller
   c. Passengers
   d. Aircraft mechanic
   e. People on the ground

10. What is the minimum speed at which an aircraft can maintain level flight?
    a. Ceiling speed
    b. Cruising speed
    c. Stalling speed
    d. Mach 1
    e. Gliding speed

11. What is the maximum operating altitude for a design of an aircraft?
    a. Stratosphere roof
    b. Service ceiling
    c. Stratosphere ceiling
    d. Overhead ceiling
    e. Upper limit

12. Which of the following is another word for aerodynamic friction or wind resistance?
    a. Lift
    b. Gravity
    c. Thrust
    d. Drag
    e. Stall

13. What is the purpose of the horizontal stabilizer?
    a. Pushes the tail left or right in line with the aircraft
    b. Levels the aircraft in flight
    c. Controls the roll of an aircraft
    d. Decreases speed for landing
    e. Decreases speed in a turn

14. Where are ailerons located?
    a. The trailing edge of a rudder
    b. The outer leading edge of a wing
    c. The outer trailing edge of a wing
    d. The inner trailing edge of a wing
    e. The empennage

15. What occurs when the induced drag on an aircraft exceeds its lift?
    a. Roll
    b. Yaw
    c. Pitch
    d. Stall
    e. Gravity

16. Which is not considered to be one of the four fundamental flight maneuvers?
    a. Landing
    b. Straight and level
    c. Turns
    d. Descent
    e. Climbing

17. What force acting upon a helicopter attempts to turn the body of the helicopter in the opposite direction of the main rotor travel?
    a. Gyroscopic precession
    b. Centrifugal force
    c. Torque
    d. Coriolis effect
    e. Centripetal force

18. What is used to increase the pitch of the main rotor at the same time at all points of the rotor blade rotation?
    a. Cyclic control
    b. Collective control
    c. Coriolis control
    d. Symmetry control
    e. Anti-torque control

19. Visual approach slope indicators are visible from what distance during clear, daylight hours?
    a. 1-2 miles away
    b. 3-5 miles away
    c. 5-10 miles away
    d. 10-20 miles away
    e. 20-25 miles away

20. Non-precision instrument runways provide what kind of guidance?
    a. Horizontal
    b. Vertical
    c. Locational
    d. Directional
    e. Multi-directional

Answer Explanations

1. B: Faster flow of air over the wing than beneath it. The air moves over the curved surface of the wing at a higher rate of speed than the air moves under the lower flat surface, which creates lift due to the aircraft's forward airspeed and enables flight.

2. B: Longitudinal. The ailerons are mounted on the trailing edges of the wings, and they are used for controlling aircraft roll about the longitudinal axis.

3. A: Lateral. Elevators are mounted on the trailing edges of horizontal stabilizers and are used for controlling aircraft pitch about the lateral axis.

4. C: Vertical. The rudder is mounted on the trailing edge of the vertical fin and is used for controlling rotation (yaw) around the vertical axis.

5. C: Aileron. The aileron is a primary flight control.

6. E: Slats. Slats are part of the wing. The tail assembly of an aircraft is commonly referred to as the empennage. The empennage structure usually includes a tail cone, fixed stabilizers (horizontal and vertical), and moveable surfaces to assist in directional control. The moveable surfaces are the rudder, which is attached to the vertical stabilizer, and the elevators attached to the horizontal stabilizers.

7. B: Skate. Depending on what the aircraft is used for, it may have skis, skids, pontoons, or floats, instead of tires, for landing on ice or water.

8. B: Semicoque. There are two types of fuselage structures: truss and monocoque. The truss fuselage is typically made of steel tubing welded together, which enables the structure to handle tension and compression loads. In lighter aircraft, an aluminum alloy may be used along with cross-bracing. A single-shell fuselage is referred to as monocoque, which uses a stronger skin to handle the tension and compression loads. There is also a semi-monocoque fuselage, which is basically a combination of the truss and monocoque fuselage and is the most commonly used. The semi-monocoque structure includes the use of frame assemblies, bulkheads, formers, longerons, and stringers.

9. A: The pilot. To ensure an aircraft is being operated properly, a pilot needs to be familiar with the aircraft's flight envelope before flying.

10. C: Stalling speed. The stalling speed is the minimum speed at which an aircraft can maintain level flight. As the aircraft gains altitude, the stall speed increases, since the aircraft's weight can be better supported through speed.

11. B: Service ceiling. The maximum altitude of an aircraft is also referred to as the service ceiling. The ceiling is usually decided by the aircraft performance and the wings, and is where an altitude at a given speed can no longer be increased at level flight.

12. D: Drag. Drag is the force generated when aircraft is moving through the air. Drag is air resistance that opposes thrust, basically aerodynamic friction or wind resistance. The amount of drag is dependent upon several factors, including the shape of the aircraft, the speed it is traveling, and the density of the air it is passing through.

13. B: Levels the aircraft in flight. The horizontal stabilizer provides for leveling of aircraft in flight. If the aircraft tilts up or down, air pressure increases on one side of the stabilizer and decreases on the other. This imbalance on the stabilizer will push the aircraft back into level flight. The horizontal stabilizer holds the tail down as well, since most aircraft designs induce the tendency of the nose to tilt downward because the center of gravity is forward of the center of lift in the wings.

14. C: The outer trailing edge of the wing. Ailerons are located on the outer trailing edges of the wings and control the roll of an aircraft.

15. D: Stall. An aircraft stall occurs at the critical AOA, where the induced drag exceeds the lift. During a stall, the wing is no longer able to create sufficient lift to oppose gravity. Stall angle is usually around 20°.

16. A: Landing. There are four fundamental maneuvers in flight: straight-and-level, turns, climbs, and descents. Every controlled flight usually includes a combination of these four fundamentals.

17. C: Torque. Torque from the engine turning the main rotor forces the body of the helicopter in the opposite direction. Most helicopters use a tail rotor, which counters this torque force by pushing or pulling against the tail.

18. B: Collective control. The collective control is used to increase the pitch of the main rotor simultaneously at all points of the rotor blade rotation. The collective increases or decreases total rotor thrust; the cyclic changes the direction of rotor thrust. In forward flight, the collective pitch changes the amount of thrust, which in turn can change the speed or altitude based on the use of the cyclic. During hovering, the collective pitch will alter the hover height.

19. B: 3-5 miles away. Visual approach slope indicator (VASI) is a light system designed to provide visual guidance during approach of a runway. The light indicators are visible 3-5 miles away during daylight hours and up to 20 miles away in darkness. The indicators are designed to be used once the aircraft is already visually aligned with the runway.

20. A: Horizontal. Non-precision instrument runways provide horizontal guidance only when there is an approved procedure for a straight-in non-precision instrument approach.

FREE Test Taking Tips DVD Offer

To help us better serve you, we have developed a Test Taking Tips DVD that we would like to give you for FREE. **This DVD covers world-class test taking tips that you can use to be even more successful when you are taking your test.**

All that we ask is that you email us your feedback about your study guide. Please let us know what you thought about it – whether that is good, bad or indifferent.

To get your **FREE Test Taking Tips DVD**, email freedvd@studyguideteam.com with "FREE DVD" in the subject line and the following information in the body of the email:

a. The title of your study guide.

b. Your product rating on a scale of 1-5, with 5 being the highest rating.

c. Your feedback about the study guide. What did you think of it?

d. Your full name and shipping address to send your free DVD.

If you have any questions or concerns, please don't hesitate to contact us at freedvd@studyguideteam.com.

Thanks again!

CPSIA information can be obtained
at www.ICGtesting.com
Printed in the USA
BVOW09s1308201216

471320BV00051B/735/P